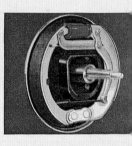

EVOLUTION • DESIGN • RACING • HOT RODDING

'40 Ford

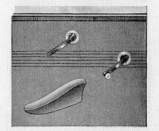

Joseph P. Cabadas

in cooperation with The Henry Ford

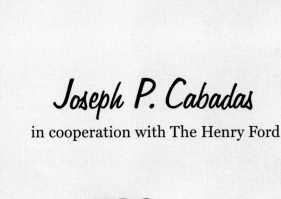

motorbooks

FORD V·8 for 1940

First published in 2011 by Motorbooks, an imprint of MBI Publishing Company, 400 First Avenue North, Suite 300, Minneapolis, MN 55401 USA

MBI Publishing Company titles are also available at discounts in bulk quantity for industrial or sales-promotional use. For details write to Special Sales Manager at MBI Publishing Company, 400 First Avenue North, Suite 300, Minneapolis, MN 55401 USA

Library of Congress Cataloging-in-Publication Data

Cabadas, Joseph, 1967-
'40 Ford : evolution, design, racing, hot rodding / Joseph Cabadas.
    p. cm.
Includes bibliographical references and index.
ISBN 978-0-7603-3761-5 (plc)
1. Ford automobile—History. 2. Nineteen forties. 3. Ford Motor Company—History. I. Title. II. Title: Forty Ford.
TL215.F7C255 2011
629.222'2—dc22

                                                                                    2010033822

Front cover: Its art deco influence and overall stylish appearance have made the '40 Ford a legend among classic car enthusiasts and hot rodders. This rodded De Luxe Coupe belongs to John Wager. © *Peter Vincent*

Frontispiece: The chevron-shaped taillights on the '40 Ford replaced the famous teardrop items that had been used on 1937–1939 models. This car is another De Luxe Coupe and belongs to Jim and Mark Westrick. © *Peter Vincent*

Back cover, left: A "typical American family" with a typical American car—in this case a 1940 Deluxe Fordor Sedan—at the 1939–1940 New York World's Fair. *The Henry Ford*

Back cover, right: A pair of street-driven hot rods—including a 1940 Ford Deluxe Coupe—face off at San Fernando Drag Strip in the late 1950s. *NHRA Museum*

Editor: Dennis Pernu
Design Manager: Kou Lor
Designer: John Sticha
Cover designer: Andrew Brozyna, AJB Design, Inc.

Printed in China

Contents

Acknowledgments

First of all, I have to thank my wife, Mary, and my family members for their support during the time it took me to research, write, fact-check, and recheck this book. Next, as an author I've been able to tell this story thanks to the trailblazing research of other writers and historians, including Allan Nevins, Frank Hill, Mira Wilkins, Ford R. Bryan, David Burgess-Wise, the countless reporters and photographers who covered the automotive industry back during the Great Depression, and others.

I would like to thank my editor, Dennis Pernu, and the others at Motorbooks for helping to guide this book to completion, including the copyediting, proofreading, layout, and marketing. Every effort has been made, with the help of all the people mentioned here, to present you with an accurate, informative, and entertaining history that captures the excitement of the past—the people who lived the tales presented here didn't know how things would turn out any more than we can know exactly what tomorrow will bring.

I owe a great deal of thanks to the staff at The Henry Ford and the Benson Ford Research Center for their never failing service, including Judith Endelman, Robert Casey, Jim Orr, Derek Moore, Carrie Nolan, Wendy Metros, Terry Hoover, Linda Skolarus, Kathy Steiner, Rebecca Bizonet, Stephanie Lucas, Jessica Miller, Elizabeth Lombardo, Linda Choo, Casey Lapworth, and Anthony Layton. I deeply appreciate the suggestions and comments made by those who helped read various drafts of the manuscript: Michael Davis; Henry Dominguez; Ford Motor Company historian Bob Kreipke; Michael Skinner with the Henry Ford Heritage Association; Michael MacSems and Sam Roberts for their knowledge about the foreign Fords; and members of the Catholic Writers Guild critique group, such as Walt Fields, Karina Fabian, and Elizia Meskill.

Others who deserve special thanks are Gena Tecos, Carrie Pruitt, and Robert Tate at the Detroit Public Library's National Automotive History Collection; Greg Sharp and Monique Valadez at the NHRA Museum; Thomas Featherstone and Mary Wallace at Wayne State University; Steve Ford "The Car Guy"; fellow Motorbooks authors, including Lindsay Brooke, Tony Thacker, and David Grant; plus members of the Ford & Mercury Restorer's Club of America, including Art Cervi, Steve Rohde, John P. Phillips, and Mark Koehler.

And I can't forget the contributions of Howard D. "Buck" Mook; David Schultz of the Glenmoor Gathering; Gene Winfield; Tom Tjaarda; Charles Maher, Keith Crain; Gary J. Mallast; Ron Watson of the Motorsports Hall of Fame; Dick Guldstrand; photographer and friend David Chapman; Thomas Murphy; Garnet R. Cousins; John Rotella; Herb Branham of NASCAR; Jackie L. Frady of the National Automobile Museum and the Harrah Collection; Shari McCullough-Arfons; Linda Ashley; Stefan Dierkes; Susan Jaszkowski with BASF Coatings; Christo Datini with the General Motors Heritage Center; Larry Erickson and Beth Marmarelli at the College for Creative Studies; Brandt Rosenbusch and Danielle Szostak-Viers with the Walter P. Chrysler Museum; Tom Kuhr; David McClelland; Ron Schneider; Larry Smith; Peter Vincent; Gene Winfield; Lorron and John A. James; plus Kirt Gross, Ken Erwood, and Helen Malakis at the Dearborn Historical Museum.

See you on the "Road to Tomorrow."

Preface

The Fabulous Forty Ford—as the 1940 Ford was called in company advertising—was an exciting and challenging subject to research and write about. Originally, I had touched upon this era in my 2004 book, *River Rouge: Ford's Industrial Colossus*, by looking more at industrial and labor history, but I knew there was more to the car development than I could cover, such as the creation of the Ford Design Department under the keen eye of Edsel Ford and Eugene "Bob" Gregorie. The '40 Ford's styling and mechanics made it one of the most attractive and desirable cars on the roads back then. One testament to the car's timeless style is its popularity with a significant segment of today's hot rodders and street rodders.

For this book, I talked to a whole new range of people, including conducting the last interview with Ross Cousins, the last surviving member of Gregorie's design staff, before his death in 2010. Other interviewees included Keith Crain, the owner of *Automotive News* and a car buff with dozens of cars in his collection (including a 1940 Ford Station Wagon); the legendary car customizer Gene Winfield; and even Dick Guldstrand (a.k.a., "Mr. Corvette"), who grew up when Ford flathead V-8s were king of the California youth market.

Along with their rich design history, 1940 Fords—and the model years that preceded them—are a glimpse of Edsel Ford's vision for the company before his death due to complications from cancer in 1943. Those years coincided with a tumultuous series of incidents, including the increasingly strained relationship between Edsel and his father, Henry Ford, the rise of the United Auto Workers union, the machinations of Ford executives in America and Europe, and, to top things off, the outbreak of World War II. It's hard to talk about just the cars without going into some of the underlying reasons why they were designed, built, marketed, and sold the way they were. Beyond this period of roughly 1937 to 1940, I've also looked at these cars' rich history in all forms of auto racing and in hot rodding.

I hope you enjoy reading this book as much as I did learning more about this era, these cars, and especially the people who built them. I've tried to give you a balanced, informative, and entertaining look at the late 1930s while, I hope, making it come alive for you via the written word and pictures.

Chapter One

Streamlining Takes Shape

The 1940 Ford represents the last of a generation of fairly compact, speedy cars that started with the 1934 Ford. Under the hood was the highly successful flathead V-8 engine that came in a 85 horsepower version, the V-8-85, or the smaller 60 horsepower "economy" size, called the V-8-60. The cars were simply and appropriately known as the V-8s and came in a variety of body styles from two-door coupes and sedans to the four-door sedan or the "woody" Station Wagon.

Designed under the auspices of Edsel Bryant Ford, president of Ford Motor Company and son of its founder, Henry Ford, the '40 Ford borrowed cues from the industry's style leader, the streamlined 1936 Lincoln-Zephyr. The Lincoln-Zephyr itself was influenced by aircraft and even boat designs.

The 1937 through 1940 Fords also were popular with Southern moonshiners because of their ability to remain nimble even while stacked with jugs of "white lightning." After delivering their products to market, the drivers wanted to see who had the fastest car and headed out to the nearest dirt track they could find, indirectly leading to the creation of the National Association for Stock Car Auto Racing (NASCAR). Out West, youths hopped up V-8s to see who was the speediest on the dry lakes of California and Nevada. After World War II, Fords gave birth to the hot rod, street rod, and drag racing movements. "Hop-ups" and car customizations existed prior to the war, but the term *hot rod* didn't become popular until 1945–1950.

Why Does the 1940 Ford Endure?

Gene Winfield, a leading creator of custom cars, hot rods, and TV and movie cars, said the 1940 Ford endures because it has a good-looking design. "Also popular is the 1939 Mercury—the first Mercury ever—that shared (a similar, though larger) body style as the '40 Ford," he said.

"There are many reasons for the '40 Ford's popularity, but the styling is what has put it over the top with many people," added Charles Maher, an automotive fine artist whose work has been featured at premier classic car shows such as Meadow Brook (Michigan) and Pebble Beach (California) Concours d'Elegances, and in car publications such as *AutoWeek*. "People found the flathead motor charming, if not exactly powerful."

"They had great engines, especially the V-8-60," countered Dick Guldstrand, owner of Guldstrand Motorsports. Although known as "Mr. Corvette," Guldstrand's earliest racing

experiences were with the Ford V-8s. "Those engines were so small and light that we made them turn 8,000 rpm in a midget. Of course, that was with the help of the talents on the West Coast, including Frank Kurtis, Emil Deidts, and Barney Navarro and others. After the V-8-60 was hopped up it probably produced close to 200 horsepower."

The V-8-60 was touted as an economy engine, at about two-thirds the size and weight of the bigger 85-horsepower V-8s. Introduced in Europe by the mid-1930s, it was used in America only for the 1937–1940 model years as Ford's answer to the six-cylinder Chevys and Plymouths. Its performance was anemic when installed in the same car bodies as the V-8-85s.

"The '39 and the '40 Fords represent the peak of prewar automotive engineering," noted Keith Crain, publisher of *Automotive News* and chairman of Crain Communications. "It wasn't until 1949 that we saw any dramatic changes."

The V-8s owed their existence to Henry Ford's decision to replace the Model A in 1932. With falling car sales and declining revenues exacerbated by the onset of the Great Depression, Ford faced a slide into insignificance if it brought out the wrong product at the wrong time.

The Short-lived Model A

When the 15 millionth Model T rolled off the Highland Park, Michigan, assembly line on May 26, 1927, it was the end of an era. Although critics called it the "Flivver" or "Tin Lizzie," many early Model T owners named their cars as if they were family members. But after 19 years of production, its popularity had waned. Ford only made 454,601 units for 1927.

The four-cylinder, 40-horsepower 1928 Ford Model A replaced the Model T, but because its design engineering wasn't completed when "T" production ended, Ford closed 30 plants nationwide, laying off more than 100,000 workers for six months. After numerous delays, including shifting home plant

Facing: Artist Charles Maher created this acrylic painting on a 34x24-inch canvas for the city of Ferndale, Michigan's 2001 Woodward Dream Cruise poster. The canvas was later exhibited at the Automotive Hall of Fame in Dearborn, Michigan, and other venues. *Charles Maher collection*

A man opens the door of a 1940 Ford V-8 De Luxe five-window business coupe in this publicity picture taken in September 1939. The De Luxe for 1940 had advances in styling, comfort, and safety, including fingertip gear shifting on the steering post, sealed-beam headlights, and softer springs in the front and rear. *The Henry Ford*

car assembly from Highland Park to the Rouge, production restarted November 1, 1927. At Edsel Ford's direction, the Model A borrowed styling cues from the much more expensive Lincoln—a trend that would continue as 1937–1940 Fords borrowed the Lincoln-Zephyr's design elements.

In 1929 and 1930, the Model A outsold all of General Motors' car brands combined. Ford's totals for 1929 were 1,356,000 vehicles versus GM's 1,315,700 units (total industry sales were a little more than 4 million units). In 1930, Ford sold 1,092,000 cars (about 40 percent of the 2.7-million-vehicle market), while GM's sales fell to a total of 937,200 units. Unlike the longevity of the Model T, the Model A's appeal was short-lived.

Threats from Chevy and Plymouth

New cars from General Motors' Chevrolet division and Chrysler's new low-priced Plymouth had features such as "floating power"—the engine on rubber mounts that greatly reduced vibration—that made Ford's car look antiquated.

Running Chevrolet was the Danish-born William S. Knudsen, a former Ford executive, who joined GM in 1921.

Under "Big Bill" Knudsen, Chevrolet beat Ford by default during Ford's 1927 shutdown. Chevy sold more than one million units, about 250,000 more cars than Ford.

The Plymouth was Walter P. Chrysler's low-priced car. A former GM executive, Chrysler created his company by merging Maxwell and Chalmers—two nearly bankrupt automakers—in mid-1925. He purchased the much larger but ailing Dodge Brothers Company three years later to gain manufacturing capacity.

As the world's economy teetered on the brink of the Great Depression, Henry Ford realized that both Chevrolet, with its new 50-horsepower six-cylinder car, and Plymouth were serious threats to the Model A. Edsel Ford and other Ford executives wanted a six-cylinder car, but Henry decided not to compete directly with GM.

"We're Going from a Four to an Eight"

One day in late 1929, "Mr. Ford"—as employees called Henry Ford—wandered to the desk of assistant engineer Fred Thoms and said, "We're going from a four to an eight because Chevrolet is going to a six. Now you try to get all the eight-cylinder engines you can."

Traveling to junkyards, Thoms found nine engines, all from higher end cars, including Cadillac, Lincoln, and LaSalle. All V-8–powered cars on the market were priced at more than $1,000. Most of the engines were complex, made from multiple castings with separate banks of cylinders bolted together, but Mr. Ford decided that his new engine would be cast *en bloc* for a car priced at less than $600.

When his engineers balked at his directives, Mr. Ford said, "Anything that can be drawn up can be cast."

Chevrolet's new six-cylinder cars robbed Model A sales even while the economy crumbled. In America, the Great Depression's roots can be traced to the Florida real estate market collapse, growing personal bankruptcies, foreclosures, and bank problems that culminated with the New York stock market crash on October 29, 1929. Consumers had nearly $2.9 billion in debt, nearly half of

which financed the record 5.6 million car and truck sales for 1929, which was blamed as a contributing factor for the Depression.

With the economy worsening, Ford hedged its bets by offering an improved version of the Model A, which became the Model B. Ironically, the company faced trouble in England where the British horsepower tax encouraged the purchase of small-engined cars. The Model A's engine was considered too big. So as the V-8 project took form, engineers in Dearborn wrestled with designing a Ford "baby" for England.

Trial and Error Solutions

Built in 1925, Ford's Engineering Laboratory Building in Dearborn was supposed to be its main research center, but Henry Ford once summed up his company's research methods saying, "We do nothing at all in what is sometimes ambitiously called research, except as it relates to our single object, which is making motors and putting them on wheels. In our Engineering

This 1940 Ford De Luxe woody Station Wagon is owned by Keith Crain, owner of Crain Communications in Detroit and editor in chief of *Automotive News*. Crain is an avid car collector who says he "likes the lines" of the 1939 and 1940 models. His car was one of about a dozen on display during the 58th annual Detroit AutoRama indoor hot rod show held February 26–28, 2010. *David Chapman collection*

Right: Henry Ford, far right, poses on March 10, 1932, with the engineering team that created the V-8 engine. In front of them is the first production 1932 V-8 Victoria. Present are chief engineer Laurence Sheldrick (third from left) with chassis engineer Joe Galamb standing next to him. Pete Martin, vice president of manufacturing, has his hand on the fender, and Emil Zoerlein is standing just behind him to the right. *The Henry Ford*

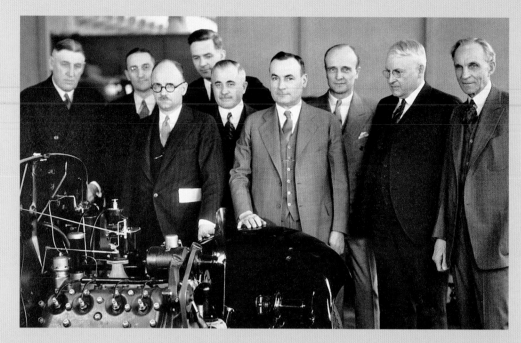

Below: Henry Ford, left, meets with engineers Emil Zoerlein (holding papers), Roscoe Smith, and William Donaldson. After learning that Chevrolet was going to introduce a six-cylinder engine for its car, Henry Ford decided in late 1929 that his competitive advantage would be to offer buyers an inexpensive V-8 engine. *The Henry Ford*

Laboratory, we are equipped to do almost anything we care to do, but our method is the Edison method of trial and error."

Trial-and-error methods prevented Ford engineers from conducting much long-term product planning. This failing hampered the launch of new cars and engines.

"No money was being spent . . . to get highly trained young men out of the universities and technical schools. Expenditures for laboratory equipment and general research facilities were made according to Henry Ford's mood and whim," noted Harold Hicks, who worked on various projects until he was discharged in 1932 and then joined Chrysler.

Mr. Ford short-circuited his company's rudimentary engineering operations when it came to developing the V-8. Also, Henry Ford's reliance on hunches was well-documented, and many of the engine's innovative features and drawbacks were more the result of his intuition than a scientific plan.

Working in Secret

In May 1930, Henry assigned the V-8 development project to Laurence Sheldrick, who was the informal head of the engineering group that guided models from the blueprint to a finished car. His team included Eugene Farkas and Cornelius Van Ranst, who handled engines; Joseph Galamb, who helped create the Model T; Dale Roeder, commercial vehicle expert; and engineer Howard Simpson. Yet, Henry Ford secretly created a second team of young engineers—including Emil Zoerlein and Don Sullivan—who made the final V-8 engine design. They worked in Thomas Edison's former Fort Myers laboratory, which had been relocated in 1928 from Florida to Greenfield Village. Henry Ford instructed Zoerlein to "keep Sheldrick out" and "not say a word to anyone" about their project even to Edsel. Before long, however, Edsel was brought in to help create the Model B and V-8 car body.

By February 1931, the first V-8 engine was running, and four months later, four engines were being tested in modified Model As.

Following Henry's dictates, Rouge foundry engineers experimented with ways to mass produce monoblock V-8 engines at a rate of 3,000 units per day. However, many of the early V-8 blocks were cast by hand with 54 cores that had to be precisely fitted into molds before the molten iron could be poured. Until the foundry figured out the proper techniques, there was a 95 percent scrappage rate of these first engines.

"The Ford Motor Company at that time was so centralized that even the methods of casting were controlled from the top," remembered engineer Frank C. Riecks. "Mr. (Charles) Sorensen controlled casting methods most of the time. However, if Mr. Ford suggested something to Sorensen, he would try every means to work it out, sometimes in spite of the fact that similar ideas proved unsuccessful."

Finally, the Rouge foundry was reconfigured, creating a conveyor that transported the molds at 100 units per hour, set

Workers in the Rouge iron foundry pour molten metal into a ladle. Following Henry's dictates, Rouge foundry engineers experimented with ways to mass-produce V-8 engines, but until they figured out how to do it, they scrapped 95 percent of the first engines. *The Henry Ford*

cores in place, and then took the assembled molds to the iron pouring line. The continuous moving operation in the foundry eliminated the backbreaking work of setting the molds, pouring the iron, and handling the castings afterward.

The Flathead

With its 16 valves located inside the V-8 block, the engine had a flat cylinder head bolted on with 21 studs, hence the nickname "flathead." Ford's V-8 had a compression ratio of 5.5:1 with 65 horsepower at 3,400 rpm and a 221-cubic-inch displacement, offering as much or more power than competitors.

Another design oddity of the Ford V-8 was that the exhaust passages ran through the block to help the engine warm up during the winter. Yet this caused overheating problems in warmer weather, until the debut of the 1937 model, which had an improved cooling system.

Henry Was the Company

As for the men who run the organization, the first point to make again and again is that only one man runs it, and he is Henry Ford," noted *Fortune* magazine in a December 1933 story. "It is a little difficult to sort out the Ford executives for the reason that Mr. Ford does not believe in titles. . . . Ask any of the executives what their jobs may be, and after a few minutes thought they might admit that they look after this or they take care of that. But never say they: 'I am the sales manager or I am the chief engineer.'"

Company executives included Edsel Ford, president and treasurer; Peter E. Martin, vice president of manufacturing; Charles Sorensen, Rouge superintendent; William C. Cowling, sales manager; Albert M. Wibel, purchasing; William Cameron, who handled publicity; Harry Bennett, the Ford Service Department; and Ernest Liebold, Henry's personal secretary. Some of Henry's lieutenants, such as Raymond C. Dahlinger, who oversaw the Ford Farms, and his wife, Evangeline Côté Dahlinger, who worked in various capacities at Ford Motor Company and Greenfield Village, were called to handle special projects.

Few industrialists have had as much influence on the world as Henry Ford. An inductee into numerous halls of fame, a 1999 Gallup poll ranked him as one of the 18 most admired people of the twentieth century. His name evokes images of the assembly line,

mass production, and the freedom of affordable transportation: Until the introduction of the Model T, 94 percent of people never traveled more than 20 miles from home.

"He was unorthodox in thought but puritanical in personal conduct. ... He hated indolence but had to be confronted by a challenging problem before his interest was aroused," Sorensen noted in his autobiography *My Forty Years With Ford*. Nicknamed "Cast Iron Charlie" for his innovations in making cast iron parts, Sorensen's powers overlapped those of Martin, his nominal boss.

Known as "Mr. Ford" even to his closest lieutenants, Henry had unrivaled control over the automaker well into World War II. This one-man rule was epitomized by a conversation he had during the 1930s with Emil Zoerlein, one of the creators of the flathead V-8. Wearing one of his ubiquitous gray hats, Ford said, "The company's board of directors and the chairman

of the board are right here, under this hat."

With his money and determination, Henry Ford created the Rouge Plant in Dearborn. Built along the banks of the Rouge River near the outskirts of Detroit, the Rouge was Ford's "home plant" and became a manufacturing showcase for a concept called vertical integration. With blast furnaces, coke ovens, steel mills, the Motor Building (an engine factory), and an assembly plant on 1,200 acres (or roughly two square miles), the Rouge was a vast factory complex that refined raw materials (iron ore, coal, limestone, and wood), made components and parts, and produced completed cars. Scrap and waste were turned into usable products ranging from alcohol, soap, charcoal, and ammonium sulphate fertilizer, to slag (which was then made into Portland cement), and Ford Benzol (a high-octane fuel alternative to leaded ethyl gasoline).

Executive roundtable luncheons were held nearly every workday in the Engineering Laboratory. Seated from left are Edsel Ford, Henry Ford, production manager Charles E. Sorensen, vice president of manufacturing Pete Martin, and vice president of purchasing Albert M. Wibel. The man with his back to the camera is unidentified. Harry Bennett, head of personnel and security, rarely attended these meetings; chief designer Bob Gregorie never did. *The Henry Ford*

Chevrolet bumped its cylinder engine up to 60 horsepower and increased it to 65 horsepower by 1933, while Plymouth's "six" equaled the V-8.

The flathead V-8 remained in production from 1932 to 1948 with various tweaks, and Ford cars adopted the larger Mercury engine after World War II. After additional modifications, the engine was produced to 1953 until it was replaced by an overhead-valve (OHV) engine. By the mid-1950s, nearly every American car company offered a V-8 engine.

A New Deal for America

The first production engine was made on March 10, 1932—three days after the Hunger March, a riot by nearly 5,000 unemployed men that occurred outside of the Rouge. Despite the clash, Henry Ford was upbeat when talking to reporters and said, "We did not invent the eight-cylinder car. What we did was to make it possible for the average family to own one. … Motor manufacturing practices will follow the trail we blazed."

The exterior of the 1932 Ford V-8 was virtually indistinguishable from the Model B. The "Deuces" had a number of bugs, including vibration problems due to inadequate engine mountings, defective pistons, high oil consumption, faulty ignition, and a malfunctioning water pump. Many of these deficiencies were corrected for the 1933 Ford, and the engine's horsepower was increased to 75 at 3,800 rpm.

Chicago car dealers saw the first 1932 Ford V-8 at the end of March, and an estimated 5 million people turned out to see sample cars when they went on display. Despite the hoopla, Ford was unable to reach full V-8 production until June. By year's end, Chevrolet sold 320,331 units to Ford's 256,867.

Later that year, Franklin D. Roosevelt won the 1932 presidential election by promising a "New Deal" for America, ushering in a number of programs that were supposed to stimulate the economy, including the National Recovery Administration (NRA). Under the NRA, each industry established a code of operations, regulated wages, and displayed the NRA's "Blue Eagle" emblem.

Although Ford Motor Company followed the codes established by the National Automobile Chamber of Commerce, Henry Ford officially rejected the NRA, earning the ire of the agency's administrator General Hugh Johnson. The general threatened to stop further federal government purchases of Ford and Lincoln vehicles, but Ford successfully waged a public relations and legal battle against the agency.

Changes in federal law also allowed workers to join unions, but corporations such as General Motors and Chrysler created so-called company unions that were answerable to management. Labor leaders refused to recognize the legitimacy of these company unions.

Major Redesigns

Ralph Roberts, a designer at Briggs Manufacturing Company in Detroit, did most of the styling for the 1932 Ford body, though Edsel Ford closely supervised and guided the process.

A year before the first production V-8 cars came off the assembly line, in January 1931, Ford added its first automotive designer to its payroll, Eugene T. "Bob" Gregorie. A native New Yorker, the 23-year-old Gregorie previously worked for Brewster, a custom car coachbuilder, and had designed yachts.

He began working directly under Edsel Ford and sketched the body design for the small 1932 Ford Model Y for England. Though Edsel was 15 years older, he and Gregorie formed a design

Hundreds of men line up outside the employment office at the Rouge's Gate 2, hoping to find work during the depths of the Great Depression on November 8, 1931. The company was in the midst of preparing the V-8 for production and prematurely announced that it would be hiring soon. *Walter P. Reuther Library, Wayne State University*

partnership that radically changed how Ford cars were styled by the later 1930s.

The 1933 Ford was a major redesign of the car. The Deuce, as far as Edsel was concerned, was an interim model; he wanted a more graceful car on a longer chassis. Edsel directed body draftsman Clare Kramer to take the styling cues of Gregorie's 90-inch-wheelbase Model Y and scale them up for a 112-inch-wheelbase car. Next, presumably after much debate with his father who abhorred product changes for change sake, Edsel convinced Henry that the company needed to make annual styling changes, so it would not fall behind GM.

The '33 Ford V-8 Model 40 had longer, sweeping front fenders that concealed the chassis and integral running boards, hiding the undercarriage. The oval Ford badge replaced the radiator cap, which was accessed under the hood, on the outer radiator shell. The model underwent more running production changes than in any other year.

Despite the improvements to the Ford, for the first time in history, Chrysler Corporation's North American sales (including Dodge, Plymouth, and DeSoto) exceeded Ford's sales. Plymouth moved firmly into the number-three sales spot, selling one out of every four new U.S. cars.

By 1934, the four-cylinder engines were dropped in North America, and Fords were exclusively powered by the V-8 that now generated 85 horsepower. Chevrolet edged out Ford by 4,500 cars for the sales lead by the end of 1934, but Ford beat Chrysler by more than 100,000 units. For the year, Ford sold 532,589 cars and 128,250 trucks versus GM's total of 852,375 cars and 157,507 trucks.

GM's Ladder of Success

The buggy-like Ford Model T was barely a step above the horseless carriage, with components chosen for functionality and ruggedness rather than with an eye for style and harmony. The conservative-styled Model A borrowed elements from the larger Lincoln, but General Motors pioneered the systematic development of future models with style as a key selling point. Its car lines slightly overlapped the next higher and the next lower priced brand so buyers could stay on the "ladder of success," purchasing a better model each time they traded in cars, without ever leaving GM's family.

Unlike GM, there was a tremendous price gap between the base model Fords and the luxury Lincolns, which attracted a far more affluent set of buyers. Another challenger was Walter

 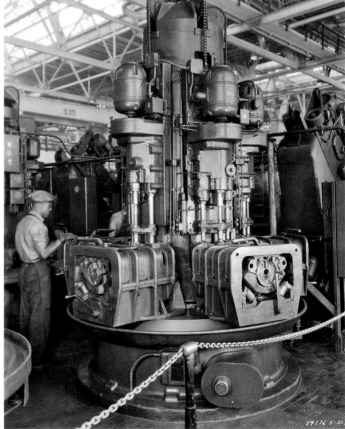

Above left: A huge multi-spindle drill press machines a V-8 cylinder block at the Rouge Motor Building (engine plant) in 1934. The stud holes for the V-8 cylinder head and valve chamber cover holes are drilled into the block at the same time. **Above right:** In the Rouge foundry machine shop in 1934, a man operates a machine that reams holes in an engine cylinder block. By the 1930s Ford employed roughly half of all African Americans who worked in the automotive industry, providing a more reliable source of income than many other industries in the North, though they still faced discrimination. *Both The Henry Ford*

A worker reaches for a V-8 engine camshaft on an overhead conveyor at the Rouge Plant. Titled *Machining Cam Shafts*, this photo was used as part of the 600-foot-long mural in the Rotunda Building that was built for the 1933–1934 Chicago World's Fair. The Rotunda was disassembled and rebuilt in Dearborn as a visitors' center for the Rouge tours. *The Henry Ford*

Chrysler, whose Plymouth brand demonstrated that low-priced cars could be beautiful and featured technological improvements such as hydraulic brakes, "floating power" where engines were placed on rubber mounts to reduce noise, vibration, and harshness; high-compression engines; improved weight distribution; and all-steel car bodies, dispensing with many wooden components then in use.

Zeppelins, Zephyr Trains Influence Car Design

When the national unemployment rate reached 26.7 percent in 1934, carmakers turned to fresh designs and new materials, including aluminum and plastics, to stimulate consumer demand. Streamlining became a popular automotive styling trend and was influenced by the graceful flowing lines of the Zeppelin airships. New trains, ships, and airplanes had rounded, tapered, and contoured lines instead of boxy, functional shapes. The style also influenced consumer goods such as toasters, stoves, irons, and even underwear—things that obviously didn't need to worry about wind resistance.

Besides airships, other influential streamline icons of the age were the Burlington Railroad's sleek *Zephyr* trains that debuted at the Chicago World's Fair. With a steel skeleton wrapped by a sweeping, flowing aluminum skin, the speedy *Zephyr* was the antithesis of earlier, boxier

locomotives. The *Zephyr* also served as an inspiration to save the Lincoln brand.

Besides the aesthetic appeal, streamlining improved fuel economy and vehicle speed by reducing wind resistance, thus providing the companies with another advertising point to sell cars.

The Fall of the Luxury Market

During the early days of the Great Depression, the custom built-to-order luxury car market peaked, but as the soup kitchen lines grew and the economic recovery remained tepid, there was a winnowing of many marginal, medium, and higher-end cars as buyers shifted to less ostentatious and more reliable vehicles. Before the start of World War II, legendary car brands such as Auburn, Cord, Cunningham, Duesenberg, duPont, Hupmobile, LaSalle, Peerless, Pierce-Arrow, Marmon, and Reo were gone (though Reo survived for a time as a truck manufacturer), along with a slew of other smaller car companies. Many other firms such as Hudson, Studebaker, Packard, and Nash barely survived. Lincoln—with models that were not much different from its 1923 car—nearly joined the ranks of the lost as its sales sagged by half to a little more than 3,100 units in 1932 and tumbled to 2,370 units in 1934. Sorensen recommended closing Lincoln, but its rescue started at Briggs Manufacturing Company.

Briggs Manufacturing was one of the largest car body builders supplying Ford, Hudson, and Packard. During the Depression the company bought LeBaron, a custom body builder for luxury cars, and made it a division of its operations. Briggs' main factory covered several acres at the Mack-Conner intersection on Detroit's east side; it had nine other plants in Michigan, Ohio, and Indiana and rented part of Ford's old Highland Park plant. Automotive pioneer Walter Briggs, who also owned the Detroit Tigers, was notorious for hard work policies, paying workers only for the time when the assembly lines were running. So, it was possible for a worker to be in the factory for ten hours but only get paid for two.

Edsel Ford frequented Briggs' main plant—located halfway between his home in Grosse Pointe Shores and Dearborn—yet Henry Ford and Charles Sorensen often felt the supplier didn't give Ford its due attention. A constant sore spot was that Briggs also supplied car bodies for Chrysler.

To gain influence, Walter Briggs hired Edsel's friend Howard Bonbright to be his liaison to the automaker and pressured designer/salesman Ralph Roberts to develop new designs for Ford.

Just as Lincoln's future looked bleak, in March 1932 Roberts sent a letter to Edsel Ford that began, "Peering into the future, projecting future trends, we have drawn our concept of the possible car of tomorrow." His letter said that the concept car was "a streamlined form" and although "at first blush our design

A worker tests a four-spoke steering wheel for a 1934 Ford at the Rouge. *The Henry Ford*

may look too unconventional to you. We would like to have you set it up somewhere in your office where it can 'season' in your estimation for a week or so." The concept car, the Sterkenberg, was the prototype of the 1936 Lincoln-Zephyr.

The Sterkenberg

Conceived by Holland-born John Tjaarda, chief designer of Briggs' LeBaron division, the Sterkenberg was a rear-engine car with fat, tear-drop front fenders, extra-wide tires, and skirted rear fenders. Tjaarda named the concept car after his family's Dutch estate. It used unit-body construction—where the body also acted as the car's frame—meaning the Sterkenberg was lighter and stronger than other cars of its size. (Unit-body construction is the same technique used on most modern vehicles.)

Prior to Briggs, Tjaarda had worked at Fokker Aircraft, created custom coach designs for Pierce-Arrow and Duesenberg, including the Duesenberg Model J, and was even at General Motors under its chief designer Harley Earl. "He had a very acute sense of humor and could tell a good story, dressing it up with a lot of flair," recalled his son, Tom Tjaarda, who inherited his father's car design abilities. (Tom Tjaarda designed the De Tomaso Pantera and several Ford Mustangs, and had a role in creating the 2008 tribute to Steve McQueen's *Bullitt* Mustang.) "He always had a future-thinking mind, always delving into new ideas and ways of designing mechanical things."

At Briggs, the Sterkenberg was the prototype for a failed international car project for North America and Europe. Instead of being produced, Tjaarda charged that Volkswagen founder Dr. Ferdinand Porsche appropriated aspects of his design for the 1938 Volkswagen experimental series. Of course, with a 25-horsepower, four-cylinder air-cooled engine, the VW "Bug" was much smaller than the Sterkenberg prototype.

Briggs made a full-size Sterkenberg ultra-streamlined wooden prototype with a functional interior. The 125-inch wheelbase car had small, fender-mounted headlights and was powered by an 85-horsepower rear-mounted, aluminum-block V-8 engine. Shown in late 1933 as the "Briggs Dream Car" to Ford executives, the car was also displayed at Ford and Lincoln dealerships along the East Coast before being exhibited at the Chicago World's Fair in the Ford Rotunda. The Rotunda was a temporary exhibition center that was reassembled in Dearborn as a visitor and display building for the Rouge Plant.

Gregorie's Redesign

Most of the public rejected the idea of a rear-engined car, but opinion samples showed that 80 percent liked its streamlined shape. Edsel Ford authorized the Sterkenberg to become the medium-priced Lincoln-Zephyr. Henry Ford okayed the Zephyr's development costs, but he and Sorensen insisted that the car have a traditional front engine and use existing Ford technology, including a transverse leaf spring suspension system and a modified Ford chassis scaled up to the Zephyr's dimensions. The initial work took place at Tjaarda's studio at Briggs, while in another part of the building Tjaarda's former teacher, Alexander Klemin, worked on the Chrysler Airflow.

For the Zephyr, Lincoln's Frank Johnson designed a new 110-horsepower V-12 engine loosely based on the Ford V-8. After styling problems with various front ends created either by Tjaarda and Briggs designer Holden N. "Bob" Koto, Edsel turned to Bob Gregorie.

Within 10 days Gregorie designed a wedge-shaped front end for the car, similar to the inverted prow of a boat. The car's wheelbase was reduced by 3 inches to 122 inches and the external body panels changed. (Altering the dimensions and panels of a prototype vehicle to adapt it for production is standard procedure even today. Many small details are changed from the basic concept until the master production model is finalized.)

Weighing approximately 3,600 pounds, the Zephyr had a top speed of 91 miles per hour and could accelerate to 50 miles per hour in about 11 seconds with an average fuel economy of 17 miles per gallon.

A Work of Art
The 1936 Lincoln-Zephyr featured a droop snoot; fender-mounted, flared-in headlights instead of the traditional pod mount; a V-shaped vertical grille with horizontal bars; a teardrop bustle; and a rear-hinged "alligator" hood where only the top of the hood was raised. Rear-hinged hoods first appeared on older Renaults and then were adopted by the Chrysler Airflows, but the 1936 Zephyr started a styling trend. With only a slight crease breaking the expanse of metal, it eliminated the traditional centerline molding down the hood. The Zephyr also had an airplane-like chrome hood ornament.

Chrysler's Airflow Flop

The first mass-produced streamlined cars were the Chrysler and DeSoto Airflows. They were conceived by Chrysler Vice President Carl Breer in 1927 after a formation of army airplanes flying over Michigan led him to consider how cars could be designed to eliminate air resistance and thus save fuel and operate more efficiently.

Consulting with airplane pioneer Orville Wright and an aircraft engineer who had built one of the country's first crude wind tunnels, Chrysler's engineers discovered that there was considerable air pressure at the front of conventional cars. Breer suggested shaping the front end more like the sloping back end, leading to the creation of the 1934–1937 Chrysler and DeSoto Airflow models.

When the Airflows debuted at the January 1934 New York Auto Show, Chrysler received an initial rush of 25,000 orders from prominent business and professional leaders in New York and California. Despite advertisements for the Chrysler Airflow claiming, "It slips through the air . . . It floats over the ground!" sales cooled. Only 11,292 Chryslers and 13,940 of the smaller DeSoto Airflows were sold by year's-end due to production problems and the Depression.

Between 1934 and 1936, Chrysler sold a total of 29,918 Chrysler and 25,237 DeSoto Airflows. Production of both cars ended after the 1937 model year.

Breer long believed the Airflows—now collectors' pieces—flopped because the

design was too far ahead of its time; his opinion was justified as cars became more rounded. Observing the Airflows' failure, Edsel Ford knew what mistakes to avoid when designing the 1936 Lincoln-Zephyr and the 1937 Ford.

Produced between 1934 and 1937, the Chrysler and DeSoto Airflows were the first mass-produced streamlined cars; however, sluggish sales spelled their end. *Chrysler Historical Collection*

(The 1936 Cord also had an alligator hood, but stylists tend to give the Zephyr the nod for changing the way hoods open on most cars.) The trunk access was through the rear passenger seat because the trunk lid only gave access to the spare tire. It had a modern interior, yet kept Ford's solid front axles and mechanical brakes.

The Zephyr's styling has had a lasting impact that is recognized decades after its debut. The Museum of Modern Art later declared the Zephyr "the first successfully designed streamlined car in America."

The car's name similarity to the *Zephyr* trains was no coincidence, noted *Automobile Topics*: "The new car resembles closely in engineering principle the new type streamlined trains, and in turn the fuselage of the most modern all-metal airplanes. The name 'Zephyr,' is thus both classic and appropriate."

When it went on sale starting at $1,275 for the two-door model and $1,320 for the four-door, the Zephyr outsold the Lincoln K by nearly 10 to 1—about 15,000 Zephyrs to 1,515 of the big Lincolns. Although the Zephyr was not a high-volume seller, it influenced Ford styling and saved the Lincoln brand as K sales nosedived to a mere 133 units by 1939.

Climbing to First

As the drama over the Zephyr played out, Briggs created the 1935 Ford and its 1936 makeover. The 1935 Ford V-8 had new body styles, fenders, grilles, hoods, and wheels. The engine was moved 8 1/2 inches forward, while changes to the passenger seating arrangement and suspension gave the car nearly perfect 50/50 weight distribution.

Ford reinforced the V-8's frame, which tended to twist and tear the bodies apart, with a riveted X-member; however, wear and tear caused the X-member to squeak. In the later 1930s, the X-members were welded to help eliminate this problem.

Although America's unemployment rate stood at 20 percent in early 1935, by the end of the year Ford's worldwide sales were 942,439 units with domestic sales of 826,519. This would be the company's best sales level until 1950. Chevrolet finished the year in second place with sales at 656,698 units, while Plymouth limped in at 382,925 units. However, in 1935, Chevy introduced its first hydraulic brake system and a new high-compression motor while Plymouth boosted engine horsepower, used better insulation, and installed superior suspensions, "shockproof" steering, and other ride and handling improvements.

Assembling 1934 Ford V-8 engines on the line at the Rouge's Motor Building. Engine improvements included replacing the Detroit Lubricator carburetor with the Stromberg 48 two-barrel that raised the engine's horsepower to 85. The new cast-steel-alloy crankshaft was more durable than the previous forged-steel shaft. *The Henry Ford*

Inspectors at the Lincoln Plant in Detroit carefully look over the big V-8 and V-12 Lincoln Ks as they come off the line in April 1934. Lincoln's sales plunged from about 6,000 units to 2,370 units in 1934, nearly spelling the demise of Ford's luxury car. *The Henry Ford*

NRA Overturned

As Ford upgraded its cars, the company's squabbles with the federal National Recovery Administration came to an end. Despite the NRA's efforts to block Ford sales to government agencies because of Henry's refusal to sign the automotive industrial codes, in March 1935 the War Department asked Ford to bid on what would be a $4 million contract to supply 4,910 cars to the Civilian Conservation Corps.

Then, in May, the U.S. Supreme Court ruled against the NRA, striking down compulsory enforcement of all industry codes. Labor frustrations built up, especially in the auto industry where there were highly seasonal employment fluctuations that corresponded to the demand for new cars.

Shortly after the court struck down the NRA, Congress passed the National Labor Relations Act (more commonly called the Wagner Act after Senator Robert F. Wagner of New York) that made union-management collective bargaining mandatory and gave labor more power to organize companies. Businesses

that tried to prevent union organizing could be charged with violating the right of free speech and assembly. General Motors President Alfred P. Sloan derided the Wagner Act as "unfair and one-sided," alleging it promoted "the exploitation of the American worker for the benefit of a comparatively few professional labor leaders responsible only to themselves."

In August 1935, the nation's largest labor organization, the American Federation of Labor (AFL), chartered the United Automobile Workers as an industrial union. The AFL was a conglomerate of 100 craft unions representing skilled tradesmen and previously made little effort to organize unskilled autoworkers.

If the UAW became successful, the AFL leaders intended to break it into traditional craft unions. More militant members, led by John L. Lewis of the United Mine Workers, hoped to organize all workers within an industry. When Lewis was prevented from talking about industrial unionism at the AFL's 1935 convention, the United Mine Workers joined seven other

Above: When Lincoln's future looked dim, Ford supplier Walter Briggs sent Ford officials a wooden prototype of a radical new streamlined car. With a rear-engine and a sloping nose, the Sterkenberg had fat, teardrop front fenders, extra-wide tires, and skirted rear fenders.
Right: This is the streamlined interior of the Sterkenberg prototype. Conceived by John Tjaarda, chief designer of Briggs' LeBaron division, the concept car was named after his family's Dutch estate. The prototype used unit-body construction, where the body acted as the frame, saving weight and trimming costs. *Both Detroit Public Library, National Automotive History Collection*

unions to form the Committee for Industrial Organization. A year later the CIO broke with the AFL, becoming a rival labor federation, and changed its name to the Congress for Industrial Organization. The UAW also joined the new militant CIO and set its sights on GM, Ford, Chrysler, and a host of smaller automakers and suppliers, including Goodyear and Briggs.

Love and Humiliation

While labor leaders squabbled, the bond between Henry Ford and his son, Edsel Ford, was fraying. The relationship between Henry and Edsel has been portrayed by some commentators as a reverse Oedipus complex, where the father sought to dominate the son. The typical storyline is that Henry purposely tormented his son so Edsel would be harder and more aggressive. Instead, Edsel acquiesced to his father's demands.

In his youth, Edsel was close to his father and possessed complementary skills and abilities. Often, the two spent several hours talking or working on one project or another. Edsel became president of Ford Motor Company on December 31, 1918, at age 25. Unlike Henry's strong-willed lieutenants, he preferred cooperation. Henry turned 70 in June 1933, well past the age that most men would have retired, but he was notorious for clinging to the public limelight. When Edsel nearly went bankrupt during the collapse of the Guardian Detroit Union Group, a bank holding company, it must have reinforced Henry's opinion

that his son wasn't ready for the job and needed to be "toughened up," an assertion made in Robert Lacey's *Ford: The Men and the Machine* and elsewhere.

Henry's toughening-up strategy included highly public displays of canceling Edsel's orders to build a bank of new coke ovens at the Rouge, and halting the implementation of new technologies on Ford vehicles such as hydraulic brakes or a six-cylinder engine.

Early hydraulic brake systems were prone to failures, but Chrysler had perfected them by the mid-1920s. Henry, though, was a proponent of mechanical brakes, using rods to connect the brake pedal to the brakes. In advertisements to dealers and in the *Ford Service Bulletins*, the company touted the "superiority" of this "steel connection" between the brake pedal and the brakes. As the V-8 car evolved, Ford was forced to switch to brake cables for the 1937 model because routing the brake rods became impractical.

With dealers crying out for more advanced systems, Edsel checked with Sorensen and Pete Martin before one executive luncheon meeting. They promised their support of the hydraulic brake proposal. The resulting exchange at that luncheon was related by Allan Nevis and Frank Hill in their 1957 work, *Ford: Expansion and Challenge 1915–1932.*

At the meeting Edsel said, "I think the time has come to take up the matter of hydraulic brakes."

One of the oddest-looking vehicles powered by modified Ford V-8 engines was the 1933–1934 Dymaxion car. With a name derived from the words "dynamic maximum tension," the front-wheel-drive, rear-engine car was designed by inventor R. Buckminster Fuller and aviation engineer and yacht designer Starling Burgess for the Chicago World's Fair. The car had only one wheel in back, which was used for steering, and could pivot 90 degrees in turns. The Dymaxion car could accelerate up to 120 miles per hour and get about 30 miles per gallon. *The Harrah Collection, National Automobile Museum*

Flustered, Henry rose from his chair and before walking out said, "Edsel, you shut up!"

Neither Sorensen nor Martin said a word in Edsel's defense. It wouldn't be until the 1939 model year that Ford offered hydraulic brakes on practically all its American vehicles.

Henry countermanded Edsel in other unpredictable ways, such as when it came to offering a Ford 6. At various times Ford dealers clamored for a six-cylinder car to counter rival products. However, Henry had built a six-cylinder engine in 1906 for the Model K and hated how it ran.

"I have no use for an engine that has more spark plugs than a cow has teats," Henry once said, but apparently he felt differently about V-8 engines. "The [V-8] is only two fours, you know."

At one point, after believing that he had his father's permission, Edsel put Ford chief engineer Laurence Sheldrick to work on a six-cylinder engine. A working prototype was soon made. Then one day Henry called Sheldrick out to the Rouge Plant to see a new scrap conveyor.

Above right: A 1936 Lincoln-Zephyr four-door sedan meets the Burlington *Zephyr* train. The Lincoln-Zephyr's design had a major styling impact on the 1937–1940 Fords, including the grille shape, fender-mounted headlights, "alligator" hood, and other streamlined elements. Using the same name as the popular streamlined *Zephyr* trains was no coincidence. *The Henry Ford*

Right: Completed 1936 Lincoln-Zephyrs are loaded into boxcars at the Lincoln Plant in Detroit on January 20, 1936. The five-passenger, four-door sedan shown has a body by Briggs, a 110-horsepower V-12 engine, 125-inch wheelbase, and weighs 3,349 pounds—all for a suggested price of $1,320. *National Automotive History Collection, Detroit Public Library*

Using an elaborate jig, a welder at the Lincoln Plant makes a Lincoln-Zephyr door frame. The luxury car was a major gamble for both Ford Motor Company and Briggs Manufacturing. *The Henry Ford*

When Sheldrick arrived at the factory, he found Edsel there with his father. Moments later the new engine was carried up the conveyor and turned into scrap.

Turning to Edsel and Sheldrick, Henry said, "Now, don't you try anything like that again. Don't you ever; do you hear?"

Ford wouldn't offer a "Six" until the 1941 model.

Rather than boosting his son, Henry's actions made many Ford managers realize that Edsel could not provide a final decision. So they went around Edsel to Henry's personal secretary Ernest Liebold, or "Cast Iron" Charlie Sorensen who ran production, Harry Bennett the personnel manager who ran security, or Raymond C. Dahlinger, who was in charge of the Ford Farms.

Sorensen's Period?

By late 1933, *Fortune* magazine reported it was well known that Edsel Ford did not like Sorensen's regime at the Rouge. The tall, handsome Danish-born Sorensen had started working at Ford in

A 1936 Lincoln-Zephyr Type 903 Two-Door Sedan is pictured alongside an American Airlines DC-3. The DC-3 was the most modern passenger plane in service at the time, and its all-metal, streamlined design influenced car designs. The Zephyr here, which also has rear quarter "butterfly" vent windows, sold for $1,275. *The Henry Ford*

1904 at age 23 as a $3-a-day patternmaker, constructing models of parts. He helped create the Rouge Plant and other factories, but was known to ruthlessly fire workers who wouldn't accept new rules after car production was shifted from Highland Park to the Rouge.

Stories circulated that Sorensen used sledgehammers and axes to wreck computing machines in the accounting department and smash the desks of supervisors who had gotten too big for their britches. Another tale had him kicking the box out from under a sitting Detroit Edison employee, knocking him to the floor, because he thought the man was a lazy Ford worker. Sorensen denied these stories, but they added to his ruthless reputation.

As Ray Dahlinger once told a Ford employee, "Sorensen's job here is to train Edsel for the big job when he can take it over. Edsel just isn't tough enough."

Sorensen's view of the company was self-serving. He stated that "1925 to 1944 was the Sorensen period," when Henry was pursuing other interests and Edsel was doing administrative work. "I was in charge of production and plant operation," he

continued, as if manufacturing was the only thing that kept a company going. He also downplayed Bennett's power grabs in the later 1930s.

As the 1930s progressed, even Sorensen acknowledged that fewer ideas came from Henry, while more came from Edsel. "The old philosophy of the car making the salesman was kicked out the window," Sorensen wrote in his autobiography. "Edsel was now bent on getting suggestions from the sales department on color schemes and accessories."

Fortune magazine noted that Edsel "has more imagination, more tolerance, a more highly developed social sense than any other man at Ford Motor Company. He is also hard-working and capable and has a sense of responsibility which will probably compel him to accept the burden of his inheritance." Although overshadowed by Henry, *Fortune* predicted that Edsel would make Ford Motor Company "a much more human organization than it is today."

Edsel made many important decisions in the 1930s, including the promotion of Bob Gregorie, designer of the 1937–1940 Fords.

Fordor and Tudor sedan bodies are visible on this silent assembly line at Ford's St. Louis assembly plant in 1935. The first body visible is a Fordor Sedan with a trunk back (the hump at the back). The 1935 Ford had new body styles, fenders, grilles, hoods, and wheels. The engine was moved 8 1/2 inches forward, while changes to the passenger-seating arrangement and suspension gave the car nearly perfect 50/50 weight distribution. *The Henry Ford*

Founding the Ford Design Department

Shortly after Bob Gregorie joined Ford, Edsel picked him to create a European-type roadster based on the 1932 Ford V-8. This car had an aluminum body fabricated at Ford's Tri-motor aircraft plant at Ford Airport, just down Oakwood Boulevard from the Engineering Laboratory in Dearborn. Again Edsel tapped Gregorie to craft one-off cars, including the two-seat Model 40 Special Speedster. Based on the 1934 Ford, the chassis was lowered by chopping a 6-inch section from the rear, turning it upside-down, and welding it back on the frame. The speedster had a special suspension, wheels, hubcaps, and fenders, plus an aluminum skin attached to a tubular frame that saved weight, while two driving lights were inspired by a Stutz, according to James and Cheryl Farrell's *Ford Design Department Concepts and Show Cars: 1932–1961.*

Painted in Pearl Essence Gunmetal Dark (i.e., gray, Edsel's favorite color), the Model 40 Special Speedster was a two-seat sport phaeton. It had a number of styling innovations that appeared on later cars such as headlights that were integrated into the body, an enclosed radiator, and no running boards.

Edsel's specialty cars used airplane tubing for frames, and each cost more than $100,000. He determined that they were too streamlined to be salable, but they were the predecessors of the Lincoln Continental prototype.

After Gregorie proved his worth as a designer, Edsel selected him to head the automaker's new Design Department in January 1935. The automaker had relied on outside suppliers for design work, but many of these companies were driven out of business during the Depression. An in-house design department gave Ford more flexibility. Sorensen suddenly became "gentle as a lamb," Gregorie noted, and helped expand the design section in the Engineering Laboratory.

With Edsel's call, 27-year-old Gregorie went from being a mere draftsman to a high-ranking company executive. "Edsel gave the order, and things had to happen," Gregorie recalled, "and he didn't want anymore dealings with Briggs as far as design was concerned."

Sorensen met with Walter Briggs while vacationing in Palm Beach, Florida. He told him that Ford would continue to buy car bodies from Briggs but would conduct its own design work. Disappointed, Briggs called Ralph Roberts about the news.

"Gather up whatever you have (which ended up being about six truckloads of design concepts and wooden models) and take it over to Dearborn," Briggs told Roberts. "We have just lost the Ford account."

Ford was the last of the Detroit Big Three to create a styling department, finally following the pattern set by General Motors years earlier to adopt yearly styling changes. When GM's Art and Colour Section (renamed General Motors Styling in January 1937) started in 1927 under the Hollywood, California–born Harley J. Earl, it quickly grew from 10 men to 50. By 1940, Earl had a staff of approximately 550 employees who had more than a dozen studios plus wood, metal, plaster, plastic, trim, and paint shops. Ford's Design Department was much smaller; it took about a year before the department had a dozen staff members.

"We were always in stiff competition with General Motors," said Ross Cousins, the last surviving member of the original Ford Design Department when interviewed shortly before his death in 2010. He joined Ford in 1938 as an illustrator. "Looking back, I'd say the cars we did looked pretty good."

Dropping to Third Place

One significant change in the auto industry was rescheduling the National Automobile Show in New York—the nation's premier display—from January to autumn 1935 to stimulate early consumer buying and thus automotive production. The idea worked and became the norm for decades.

By 1936, Ford was fully committed to annual style changes. Ford dropped spoke wheels in favor of pressed-steel wheels; the radiator grille and vertical louvers were rounded, blending into the side panels. One of the more radical changes was the use of soybean-based plastic for small parts and window trims, which resulted from research conducted in a laboratory at Greenfield Village. Soybean-based parts reduced the car weight by about 20 pounds.

A 1935 editorial cartoon by Henry Costello spoofs Ford's dispute with the National Recovery Administration (NRA). When Ford refused to sign onto the federally backed automotive industry standards, the NRA unsuccessfully tried to block Ford and Lincoln sales to government agencies. *The Henry Ford*

Despite the minor technical improvements and the publicity gained by winning the 1936 Monte Carlo Rally, Ford's U.S. market share shrank to 22 percent, behind GM at 43 percent and Chrysler at 25 percent. It was a significant drop for Ford, which had sold nearly one out of every three new cars in America in 1935.

Ford's woes were compounded on the cash side. By midsummer 1936, GM earned $88 million for the second quarter of the year, which the *New York Times* reported as the largest amount earned by a corporation since the 1929 stock market crash. However, Ford's profits for the entire year were only $17 million.

Part of Ford's cash crunch could be attributed to the factory expansions at the Rouge and elsewhere in North America and overseas. Spending money on new plants and equipment didn't concern Henry Ford very much, especially since there were no shareholders outside of the family to worry about. As Sorenson recalled in his autobiography, *My Forty Years with Ford*, when Ford spent $50 million to develop the V-8, Henry once told him, "Charlie, we have too much money in the bank. That doesn't do that bunch in the front office any good.

When they look at it they become self-satisfied, and I know they are getting lazy."

A decade earlier Ford led the automotive industry, but by the mid-1930s its products trailed the competition. Chevrolet and Plymouth cars featured engineering advances that gave drivers better rides, safety, and handling. The mechanical brakes on the 1936 Ford tended to deteriorate when the wheels got damaged and the left-side brakes pulled harder than the right side. They also made groaning noises and would seize up. Ford engines tended to overheat in hot weather; their high-mounted fuel pumps also vapor-locked when temperatures rose under the hood.

Ford experimented with new manufacturing methods to improve quality and to lower costs. It worked on rust-proofing metal parts and developed cast-steel crankshafts superior in endurance and strength to forged steel.

Still, Henry Ford turned a deaf ear to car dealers who wanted a six-cylinder engine to counter the offerings from Chevrolet and Plymouth. Instead, the company brought out a new "economy" 60-horsepower V-8 for 1937. Ford cars also took on a radically new appearance as Gregorie's styling department borrowed elements from the successful Lincoln-Zephyr.

A panoramic view of the Rouge Plant in Dearborn, Michigan, taken from the northwest in 1940. In the foreground is the Rotunda, an exhibition and visitor center that resembled a nested set of gears from above. On the opposite side of Schaefer Road from the Rotunda is the Administration Building, then a field and train lines (part of which is where modern day Interstate 94 runs), and then the Rouge's steel mills and factories. *The Henry Ford*

A 1936 Standard Fordor Sedan body is lowered onto a chassis. Note how strong the welded steel must be as the body is lifted by its doors and roof without distorting its shape. The style of the Fords would change radically the following year. Styling improvements for the 1936 models included pressed-steel wheels, an altered radiator grille, and rounded vertical louvers that blended into the side panels. *The Henry Ford*

Chapter Two

Radical Departures

Ford Motor Company debuted its new 1937 cars in a $500,000 extravaganza unprecedented in its 33-year history. For the first time ever, it invited dealers from across the United States and Canada—some came from Europe and Asia—for a two-day presentation on November 6 and 7, 1936. Chartering 41 trains, including a deluxe 15-car Pullman train for the New York dealers, and renting some 4,700 hotel rooms, Ford brought about 8,000 people to the Motor City.

On a chilly November 6 morning, a fleet of 325 buses shuttled dealers to the Michigan State Fair Grounds at Detroit's outskirts near the intersection of Woodward Avenue and Eight Mile Road. In the Coliseum arena, a 100-foot diameter spiral stage dominated the center floor. Edsel Ford welcomed the dealers, then Ford sales director, William C. Cowling, and his assistant, John R. Davis, gave them a goal of selling 1.3 million vehicles in 1937. Although Ford's domestic sales for the year would fall far short at 765,933 units, with a total of 848,608 cars sold worldwide, it was one of the company's best years since 1929.

Spotlights shone down on the arena floor, and the dealers buzzed with excitement as a huge V-8 emblem rose from the center of the stage. Dressed as a sprite, a 12-year-old girl with golden curls unwound herself from the emblem and ran to the side of the stage. Hundreds of children of Ford employees appeared dressed as gnomes carrying huge posters of car components. Converging to the center of the platform, the children threw the "parts" into an immense cauldron and stirred the "magical brew" with paddles. A red flame and steam arose and the lights dimmed. Suddenly an elevator brought a 1937 Ford Club Coupe into view to the dealers' raucous cheers. As new models came up the coiled ramps, Cowling and Davis described each one.

When Henry Ford appeared, the dealers gave him a 15-minute standing ovation. Rounding out the day, the dealers presented Henry Ford with a seventeenth-century windmill that had been moved from Cape Cod and was reinstalled at Greenfield Village. Then they returned to the Coliseum for a vaudeville show, music by Fred Waring and the Pennsylvanians, and dinner with a bottle of wine on every table. Knowing of Henry's opposition to alcoholic beverages, one dealer exclaimed, "Oh, boy, this is a liberalized company!"

On November 11, 1936, the Ford display of '37 models opened at the Hotel Astor in New York City, concurrent with the New York Auto Show that was sponsored by the Automobile Manufacturers Association. (Henry Ford generally refused to participate in AMA programs because he thought it was controlled by General Motors.)

Radically Streamlined Fords

Radically streamlined when compared to the previous Fords, the 1937 cars were the first created by Bob Gregorie's new Design Department and had a number of new features, including a 60-horsepower V-8 engine, a higher capacity water pump, and cast-alloy steel pistons.

Copying the Lincoln-Zephyr's exterior styling cues, the Fords had all-steel "teardrop" bodies, including an all-steel top, an alligator hood, and a sharp-nosed and rakish front with a radiator grille that curved deeply into the hoods' sides. The headlights were molded into the crowned front fenders, an exceptional design feature because most cars had torpedo-shaped lights mounted on the radiator shell or the fenders.

The Fords came in the De Luxe—equipped with the 85-horsepower engine, a chromed grille, and a few other amenities—plus the Standard, which had the V-8-60 as standard equipment (the V-8-85 was an option) and a plain painted grille. Another significant design change was the one-piece all-steel top. Ford had lagged behind competitors GM and Chrysler, which had promoted their "turret top" cars for more than a year. Prior to the 1937 model, Ford didn't have steel presses large enough to stamp a one-piece steel top, so its closed cars used a fabric insert, supposedly to cut weight and reduce "body drumming."

Available in 11 body styles, the '37 Fords' suggested manufacturer's retail prices started at $480 for the Standard five-window Coupe, ranging up to $790 for the De Luxe Convertible Sedan. Five of the most popular body styles were available with or without De Luxe equipment, including the

Facing: This was a typical scene along the chassis assembly line on the ground floor of Rouge "B" Building in 1937. Here the engine, transmission, radiator, front fenders, axles, running boards, and many other components have already been installed. *The Henry Ford*

Coupe, Tudor Sedan, Tudor Touring Sedan, Fordor Sedan, and Fordor Touring Sedan. The remaining styles were only available on the De Luxe, including the Roadster, Phaeton, Club Coupe, Club Cabriolet, and Convertible Cabriolet. Having fallen out of favor, the Roadster and Phaeton lost their unique cowl rolls and slanted dashes, becoming windowless versions of the Cabriolet and Convertible Sedan.

The 1937 cars had a V-shaped windshield, hinged at the top so it could be opened for ventilation. The Standard had a single windshield wiper on the driver's side, while the De Luxe had dual wipers (unlike modern cars, the wipers on the closed cars were mounted at the top of the windshield rather than the cowl). There were more colors, options, and accessories, including seat covers, an electric clock, visor vanity mirror, a deluxe steering wheel, plus hub and spoke covers. Cars equipped with the optional radio had an adjustable outside antenna hung down the middle of the windshield; in the center of the grained wood instrument panel was a large, illuminated dial near the ashtray.

To give drivers an unobstructed view of the gauges, the Fords featured the new "clear vision" three-spoke steering wheels with the top two spokes more or less horizontal. All closed body styles had the new "clear-vision ventilation system" (like a modern car, the vents could be directed to defrost the windshield). The seats were wide with pillowed upholstery and wide pleats.

Company advertising noted that the cars' "new cable and conduit control 'soft easy action brakes,'" provided "the 'safety of steel' from pedal to wheel." Although the brakes were improved when compared to previous Fords, hydraulic brakes were the industry's norm.

Other improvements included a better steering gear and numerous small upgrades, such as body and engine rubber mountings to cut down on squeaks from metal-to-metal contact.

An Improved "85" and the Thrifty Sixty

The V-8-85's aluminum heads were redesigned and the water pumps were moved to the upper front of the engine block so

One of the nearly 8,000 people who attended Ford's first-ever national dealers' meeting, held at the Michigan State Fair Grounds, holds up an issue of the *Detroit Times* announcing the new 1937 models. *The Henry Ford*

On the chilly morning of November 6, 1936, a fleet of 325 buses shuttled nearly 8,000 dealers to the Ford show at the Michigan State Fair Grounds. There, inside the Coliseum, a spotlight illuminated a huge V-8 emblem that rose from the center of the stage (inset top left). Moments later, hundreds of children dressed as gnomes carried huge posters of car components up ramps to the stage (inset lower right). The children threw the parts into a cauldron that spewed red flame and smoke before revealing a white 1937 Ford De Luxe Coupe to the cheers of the dealers in the Coliseum arena. *The Henry Ford*

An engineering picture of the welded steel body of a 1937 Ford Standard Fordor Sedan. Briggs Manufacturing Company of Detroit supplied many of the passenger car bodies for Ford during the late 1930s. One of the largest body builders of its day, Briggs also supplied Chrysler, Hudson, and Packard. In 1929 it erected a plant at Dagenham, England, to make Ford bodies in Europe. *National Automotive History Collection, Detroit Public Library*

they would push water through the system instead of siphoning it, improving cooling. The engine's new combustion and domed pistons reduced engine knock, but the compression ratio dropped to 6.12:1. Despite the Stromberg 97 carburetor (so named because of its 0.97-inch venturi), horsepower remained steady.

The 60-horsepower V-8 engine was Ford's answer to the "sixes" offered by its competitors. Marketed as an economy engine, the V-8-60 could get 22 to 27 miles per gallon while still attaining a top speed of 75 miles per hour. Davis, who became sales manager after Cowling's retirement in December 1936, started the "thrifty sixty" sales campaign to promote the low operating costs of the V-8-60 versus any previous Ford.

With a 136-cubic-inch displacement, the V-8-60 was two-thirds the size of the larger 221.6-cubic-inch V-8-85. It had an L-head with a 2.6-inch bore and a 3.2-inch piston stroke and a compression ratio of 6.6:1—the best revving of any of Ford's engines. The rated peak horsepower was at 3,500 rpm, but the horsepower curve was not reached even at 4,000 revolutions per minute.

PICTURES

DETROIT PUBLIC LIBRARY
AUTOMOTIVE HISTORY COLLECTION

1937 Ford V8, Model 60

Popular Automobile Colors

With America recovering from the worst depression in its history, and with a more hopeful outlook for the future, car buyers were "turning toward gayer hues, if exhibits at shows throughout the country can be an indicator of desire," *Automobile Topics* reported in December 1936. Colorists of various car manufacturers, with the assistance of the Duco Color Advisory Service, brought out brighter metallic colors, with new shades never before seen on automobiles.

Black, which had been the top color for many years, fell to fourth place for 1937 models, with three exhibitors at the New York Auto Show not bothering to display a black car. Blue in varied shades was the most popular; next came gray, also in several shades, including gunmetal and ivory. Other popular colors were maroon, brown, beige, cream, tan, and red.

From spring 1934 through 1940, Ford offered special colors to entice buyers into the showroom. The Easter Color program started

with a sprinkling of two-tone cars in silver or cream as part of the Chicago World's Fair promotion. Special promotional colors for the 1935 San Diego Exposition were Palm Beach Gray, Rust Brown Metallic, and Slate Green.

In 1936, Ford officially began offering special spring colors between March and mid-May, along with complementary pinstripes. Special colors included Desert Sand, Bambalina Blue, Light Fast Maroon, Armory Green, and Garnet.

Powering English- and French-built Fords, some of which were smaller than American cars, the "60" demonstrated remarkable endurance and won numerous awards in competitions against European makes. Despite being smaller, the "60" only cost $4 less to manufacture than the larger V-8, so the company did not see any significant savings in the United States.

During informal discussions with reporters, Henry said the smaller V-8 engine was close to his heart: "When we first developed the V-8, I told the engineers to start work on a smaller motor, about two-thirds the size of the one they developed for the original V-8. By golly, that's the way it turned out by exact scale."

Called "my wild Irishman" by Henry Ford, Don "Sully" Sullivan was primarily responsible for creating the V-8-60. Starting at Ford in 1928, Sullivan also developed the intake manifolds for the Miller-Ford racing cars that lost the 1935 Indianapolis 500.

"There isn't a lot of paperwork available on why [the V-8-60] was created," said Tom Kuhr of Dearborn, Sullivan's grandson. "When my grandfather was asked about it, he'd give you a look that you were crazy and say that there wasn't a question of how and why; it's just what Henry wanted done. They didn't ask why."

Commercial Cars and Trucks

In addition to its passenger cars, Ford offered the Station Wagon as a utility vehicle, primarily for commercial use. The coupe was also offered with a special pickup box as a dealer-installed accessory for sales representatives who carted samples or bulky merchandise. Replacing the regular rear deck lid, the pickup box had a floor made of seasoned wood protected against wear by steel skid strips; the sides and tailgate were all steel.

Along with an improved "85," the V-8-60 was offered across Ford's commercial truck line but proved to be underpowered when it was installed on the ton-and-a-half truck chassis—especially with the stake truck body, which weighed 4,400 pounds empty. The "60" was dropped from heavy truck use after the 1937 model year.

Ford's 1937 trucks were conservatively styled on the outside with a shield-shaped vertical grille with horizontal bars, though the hood louvers and radiator shell were new. They were offered in a wide range of body styles—including pallet, stake, and dump truck bodies—wheelbases, axle ratios, transmissions, tire sizes, and special and deluxe equipment options.

One improvement on the trucks, which the passenger cars didn't have, were longitudinal springs for the rear end. Since Henry Ford didn't pay as much attention to commercial vehicles as the cars, Ford executive Dale Roeder was able to introduce such various changes on trucks before they found their way to passenger cars.

A Place for the Design Department

The 1937 Ford and subsequent models up through 1942 were the fruits of the Ford Design Department under the control

Radically streamlined when compared to the previous Fords, the 1937 Ford's style was the first fruits of Bob Gregorie's new Design Department. Straddling a ditch, this driver seems to demonstrate the Ford's ability to take on heavily rutted terrain with its transverse leaf spring suspension. *The Henry Ford*

Workers prepare the 60-horsepower, V-8 engines for testing at the Rouge motor building. Each newly assembled engine, along with its transmission, was connected to oil and water lines. An electric motor spun the engine until its mechanical friction was ready for road usage. Inspectors also looked for oil and water leaks. *The Henry Ford*

of Bob Gregorie. Its home for much of the 1930s and the 1940s was the southwest corner of the Engineering Laboratory, about a quarter-mile north of the Ford Airport in Dearborn. That corner of the building was special to longtime Ford employees because it was where Henry Ford once held impromptu old-fashioned dances. Instead of altering the space, the Design Department used temporary partitions of yellow oak and frosted glass.

Constructed in 1924, the Engineering Laboratory was designed by architect Albert Kahn who was responsible for a number of other Ford projects including the Highland Park, Rouge, and Gorky plants (the latter, in the ancient city of Nizhny Novgorod, was a joint venture between Ford and the Soviet Union).

Originally, the Engineering Laboratory was 800 by 200 feet. The vast polished maple floor was lit by skylights. Edsel Ford's sons—Henry II, Benson, and William Clay—would sometimes appear at the building on Saturday mornings and buzz around the vast floor on the powered floor polishers to the consternation of the maintenance crew. On the building's facade were the names of 21 scientists and inventors, including Bell, Marconi, Edison, Diesel, Curie, Newton, Pasteur, and

Ford Motor Company's first chief designer, Eugene T. "Bob" Gregorie, created several special cars for Edsel Ford. His first major assignment was designing the small English Model Y. *The Henry Ford*

The names of 21 scientists and inventors are chiseled in stone above the main windows of the Albert Kahn–designed Engineering Laboratory. The Ford Design Department was housed here from the mid-1930s until after World War II. *The Henry Ford*

Galileo. The building's other appointments included mahogany woodwork, brass hardware, and marble. Henry and Edsel Ford, Charles Sorensen, and other Ford executives marked their heights on a beam there in 1938.

By that year, Gregorie's staff had grown to about 25 men who earned an average of 65 to 75 cents per hour; they were styling all Ford vehicles by 1939 while having created the 1939 Mercury, the 1940 Lincoln-Zephyr Continental Cabriolet, and even a tractor at Henry Ford's request. Despite all of its responsibilities, the Design Department's staff remained under 100 before the outbreak of World War II.

"Gregorie was able to balance the needs of a volume product and instill it with very attractive qualities that had a broad appeal to them," noted Larry Erickson, former chief designer of the award-winning 2005 Ford Mustang and now chair of transportation design at Detroit's College for Creative Studies. Erickson said that Edsel brought "a very personal approach to the elegance of design, and I still think Ford tries to do that."

False Security—Labor's Secret Weapon

Even as the auto companies brought out their new 1937 models, they were engulfed with labor unrest. Industry leaders and analysts felt a false sense of security, noting that a fraction of workers were unionized—the fledgling United Auto Workers union only had 25,000 members while three other independent unions had a combined 20,000 members on their rolls. Strategists at the Congress of Industrial Organizations intended to organize the union-busting steel industry and the automakers' suppliers rather than take on the automakers themselves. Detroit was known as one of the premier "open shop" towns in the nation, where an employee did not have to belong to a union as a precondition of being hired or continuing to be employed in a company. Yet seven years of Depression, pay cuts, assembly-line speed ups, harsh work rules, and inconsistent employment had eroded many people's anti-union sentiments.

The CIO radically departed from labor's usual practice of declaring a strike in advance and setting pickets outside a

The 1937 Fords were available in 11 body styles, including four open-top cars such as the De Luxe Roadster pictured here, possibly on Dearborn's Village Road outside of Greenfield Village (Henry Ford's amusement park to the pre-automotive age). Having fallen out of favor, the Roadster and Phaeton lost their unique cowl rolls and slanted dashes, becoming windowless versions of the Cabriolet and Convertible Sedan. *The Henry Ford*

factory. Instead, strikers checked into a plant as normal but then stood or sat by their machines and did nothing. Due to the possibility of damaging equipment, companies were reluctant to roust sit-down strikers from the factories.

Employers claimed that sit-down strikers were guilty of illegal trespassing, and a 1939 U.S. Supreme Court ruling eventually outlawed such strikes.

On December 26, 1936, a strike started at General Motors' Fisher body plant in Cleveland. Four days later the sit-down strike expanded to GM factories in Flint and then the Cadillac and Fleetwood factories in Detroit while an epidemic of sporadic smaller strikes disrupted steel, glass, and parts suppliers and even Ford's Lincoln plant in Detroit. While the GM strike dragged on, a sit-down strike hit Briggs in early January 1937, threatening Ford production. Harry Bennett, the Ford executive in charge of plant personnel and security, said he could help the union and Briggs settle the strike. Bennett apparently had befriended UAW President Homer Martin. Some have suggested this was an attempt by Bennett to wean Martin from the union. When Ford executive Charles Sorensen told Walter Briggs of Bennett's idea, the auto supplier insisted that

he would run his business his way, but Martin countered with a demand: "No meetings unless Bennett sits in."

As Sorensen argued with Briggs, Henry Ford drove to Highland Park and mingled with the strikers, telling them that the automaker was investigating their complaints.

Top: A woman sits in the driver's seat of a 1937 Ford De Luxe, which has plenty of headroom. The instruments are arranged in front of the driver and the starter button is located on the wood-grain dash.
Above: The 1937 De Luxe Phaeton was a windowless version of the Convertible Sedan, sharing the same sheet metal. A cap was welded to the top of the doors to hide the window slots. *Both The Henry Ford*

The 60-horsepower V-8 engine initially was offered across Ford's commercial truck line. This is a special demonstrator truck — possibly a 131 1/2-inch wheelbase stake truck — that was used to show how economically the engine ran. The V-8-60 proved to be underpowered when installed on the ton-and-a-half truck chassis, however. The engine was dropped from heavy truck use after the 1937 model year. *The Henry Ford*

Ford's Station Wagon began evolving from being a purely commercial vehicle, but it wasn't yet promoted as a passenger car. The 1937 wagon had a utilitarian interior, but safety-glass windows had replaced the snap-on window curtains used on earlier models. Between 1934 and 1939, the Murray and Baker-Rauling companies assembled wagon bodies from wooden parts fashioned at Ford's Iron Mountain Plant. *National Automotive History Collection, Detroit Public Library*

Determined to keep Ford's security chief from interfering in the negotiations, Walter Briggs turned to his treasurer, Howard Bonbright, a friend of Edsel Ford, to ask Edsel to call off Bennett. Back in Dearborn, Edsel argued with his father over the Briggs affair, and Sorensen took responsibility for the mess-up in communications.

"It was a bad moment for Edsel," Sorensen wrote in his autobiography. "He learned that Henry Ford and I had been in the Briggs plant and was shocked to think his father faced that mob."

Upset at Briggs' tactics, Henry Ford pulled Sorensen aside and ordered him to "pull that bodywork out of Briggs. Do it as quick as you can. You can handle it; let no one stop you."

Although the Briggs strike lasted only 12 days, it caused a permanent break between the body manufacturer and Ford. The Rouge Pressed-Steel Building was enlarged so Ford could build

Left: Various 1937 grilles travel on an overhead conveyor toward the final assembly line while men inspect and repair them. An upright truck grille is visible at lower right. *The Henry Ford*

Below: A 1937 Ford De Luxe Business Coupe—complete with optional side mirrors and passenger-side key lock—pulls a work trailer. This vehicle was owned by Simonds Saw and Steel Company of Massachusetts, a manufacturer of industrial cutting tools. As the United States emerged from the Great Depression, trailering became popular for work and pleasure. Crude, homemade trailers gave way to streamlined, factory-built trailer coaches that went well with the streamlined cars that pulled them. *National Automotive History Collection, Detroit Public Library*

its own car bodies. By 1941, Briggs lost all of its domestic Ford business and became dependent upon Chrysler.

A Strong, Aggressive Man

The 44-day General Motors sit-down strike ended in February with the giant automaker's grudging recognition of the UAW. A contract was signed, but a series of sit-down strikes, started by individual workers with the union stepping in to orchestrate the outcomes, spread like wildfire across the industry. Chrysler, Hudson, Reo, and Studebaker capitulated to the UAW.

Due to the right combination of circumstances, the unions enjoyed unprecedented success in the car industry. In April 1937, the U.S. Supreme Court upheld the Wagner Labor Relations Act, forcing companies to comply with its provisions. The Roosevelt administration also had established the National Labor Relations Board, which operated on the theory that unfair labor practices obstructed interstate commerce.

Henry planned to beat the unions and the NLRB. After an executive luncheon, he instructed Sorensen and Edsel not to meet with any union officials or to publicly discuss labor matters, explaining, "I've picked someone to talk to the unions. I want a strong, aggressive man who can take care of himself in an argument, and I've got him. He has my full confidence, and I want to be sure that you, Edsel, and you, Charlie, will support him."

When Sorensen drove Henry and Edsel to his office, he found that Mr. Ford's negotiator was none other than Harry Bennett. Sorensen said he wasn't surprised by the choice, but noted that Edsel "tightened up."

A former navy diver and professional boxer, Bennett had joined Ford in the late 1910s. Stocky and only 5 feet 7 inches tall, by 1927 he was head of the Rouge Plant's personnel department

Bennett was charged with protecting Edsel and Edsel's children from abductors after the Lindbergh baby kidnapping. To keep alert to any threats against the Ford family, Bennett developed relationships with numerous gangsters, including Joe Tocco, a rum runner who called Bennett "Boss" and was gunned down in 1938; Chester LaMare, who was given a lucrative concessionaire's contract in the Rouge before he was rubbed out in 1931; and the Purple Gang, who were involved with the 1929 St. Valentine's Day Massacre in Chicago.

Along with his mob connections, Bennett cooperated with the FBI, knew J. Edgar Hoover, and had contacts within Michigan's state government and beyond. His power base at Ford was the innocuous sounding Service Department.

Established in 1922, the Service Department handled plant security, cleanliness, and safety, but Bennett also oversaw the company's system of about 8,000 spies who kept an eye on workers with "Bolshevik" tendencies. Troublemakers could be fired or allegedly beaten as an example to other Ford workers. Bennett also created the Knights of Dearborn to keep track of activities outside of the Rouge. Operating from his basement office in the administration building, Bennett had an electronic board that flashed alerts from his operatives and had easy access to the executive garage so he could bring in people for secret meetings, whether legitimate or questionable.

With his new directive to keep the union out of the company, Bennett gained new authority to hire, fire, and transfer nearly anyone on the company payroll. The Service Department grew to 800 members whose ranks included former boxers and policemen, ex-baseball players, recently released criminals, and even members of the University of Michigan football team.

Ford offered a special dealer-installed aftermarket pickup box for the 1937 Ford De Luxe and Standard Coupes. Replacing the regular rear decklid, the pickup box had a tailgate with drop chains and a floor of seasoned wood with steel skid strips to protect against wear. The box was for owners who needed passenger car comfort and commercial car capacity. *The Henry Ford*

Henry Ford visits Harry Bennett's office in the basement of the Administration Building adjacent to the Rouge Plant. Bennett was in charge of personnel and running plant security through the Ford Service Department, where he became feared and loathed by union organizers. Ruthless, Bennett once said that he was closer to Henry than Edsel because he was completely loyal and did what Henry wanted done.
The Henry Ford

The first test of Bennett's ham-handed tactics blew up into a public relations fiasco.

Battle of the Overpass

UAW leaders Walter Reuther and Richard Frankensteen and others began action to organize the Rouge. On May 26, 1937, about 60 UAW organizers arrived at the gates of the mighty Rouge to pass out leaflets to workers during shift changes. The union leaders asked for and received permission from the city of Dearborn for this activity, though a Ford worker had warned the city council that there would be trouble.

Waiting for the main group of leafleteers, Reuther, Frankensteen, and several others walked onto the pedestrian bridge over Miller Road at Gate 4, the principal workers' entrance into the east side of the factory complex. They briefly posed for photographs by a newspaper cameramen when a contingent of 35 to 40 brawny men, including two professional wrestlers, a boxer, and several Ford servicemen, descended on the UAW leaders.

Even as the union men turned to leave, other guards blocked their path and suddenly attacked.

Top left: UAW organizers Robert Kanter, Walter Reuther, Richard Frankensteen, and J. J. Kennedy watch as Ford servicemen approach on the Rouge Gate 4 overpass on the morning of May 26, 1937. **Top right:** Moments later, the servicemen attack and Frankensteen is seen with his coat pulled over his head. **Bottom:** Kanter, Frankensteen, and Reuther are shown after the incident, which became infamously known as the "Battle of the Overpass." *Walter P. Reuther Library, Wayne State University*

Although bank robbers such as Bonnie Parker and Clyde Champion Barrow brought notoriety to the V-8s for using them as fast getaway cars, Ford played up how police used their cars. Here, Sheriff Homer Sylvester (right) of Cass County, Nebraska, and his brother, Deputy Sheriff Cass Sylvester, are pictured with their black 1937 Standard in which they captured fleeing bank robbers who had killed an FBI agent during a Topeka, Kansas, shootout in April 1937. *The Henry Ford*

"The men picked me up about eight different times and threw me down on my back on the concrete," Reuther recalled, "kick(ing) me in the face, head, and other parts of my body. . . . They threw me down the stairs . . . drove me to the outside of the fence, about a block of slugging and beating and hurling me before them."

The ensuing Battle of the Overpass, as the incident became known, lasted only about a minute, but dozens of UAW members, including several women, were treated for lacerations and multiple bruises; one man's back was broken and another died months later due to complications from being beaten. Bennett insisted that the Service Department had no role in the incident.

Although there had been many other more bloody clashes between industrialists and labor, the Battle of the Overpass occurred in front of the press, and the story spread nationwide, tarnishing Ford's reputation.

Best Sales Year Since 1929

Although the union's drive to organize the Rouge Plant was fraught with drama and historical significance, there were still cars to sell. The job of boosting Ford's market share fell to John R. Davis, who succeeded Cowling as general sales manager in December 1937. Cowling had spent six years in the job as Ford's North American market share plunged from first to third; well respected by Ford dealers, Jack Davis was eager to arrest the fall.

Competition was keen in the low-price field. Plymouth had built its two millionth car in 1936, reaching that record in less time—eight years—than any previous automaker. Although Henry wanted to have the least expensive car on the market, Ford's Fordor Sedan was actually $3.67 more than Plymouth's competing model.

Under Davis, Ford recorded another milestone as the 25 millionth Ford car since the company's founding in 1903—and the millionth 1937 Ford V-8—was assembled on July 9, 1937, in a celebration that brought Henry and Edsel together on stage at the Rotunda. The 1937 total did not include Ford's V-8 production in Canada, Lincoln and Lincoln-Zephyr production, or totals at Ford's overseas companies. The Ford brand also gained a boost when a V-8 won a second Monte Carlo Rally in Europe in 1937.

On the surface, the economy worked in favor of the auto industry. Despite strikes, *Ward's Automotive Reports* noted that automobile sales during the first three months of 1937 were on track to have the best sales year since 1929, with 1.27 million cars sold compared to 1.54 million in 1929 (up 13 percent from 1936's first-quarter sales).

U.S. manufacturing employment reached 1929 levels by April 1, 1937, with approximately 11 million people on the payrolls, though there were still an estimated 3 million to 10 million people out of work. Auto sales and wages were approaching pre-Depression peak levels, but there was a fundamental weakness in the economy. America slipped back into recession before the year's end.

Although hydraulic brakes were industry standard by 1937, Ford still used mechanical brakes and offered displays such as this to tout the supposed "'safety of steel' from pedal to wheel." Ford wouldn't catch up with the industry until the 1939 model year. *The Henry Ford*

Ford tried to make practical use of nearly every manufacturing byproduct. Here, a 1937 De Luxe Tudor Touring gets a refill at a Ford dealership. Benzol, a derivative of bituminous coal used in steelmaking operations at the Rouge, was marketed as an alternative to gasoline. *The Henry Ford*

Transverse Leaf Springs

Some mechanical equipment on the Ford V-8s—such as transverse leaf springs and its torque-tube driveshafts—were considered out of date by the late 1930s.

One of the simplest forms of suspension, the automotive leaf spring evolved from those used on horse-drawn carriages and wagons. On vehicles that carry heavy loads, such as pickup trucks, leaf springs help spread the load more widely over the chassis, reducing vibration from

Transverse leaf springs, which run parallel to the axle, were used widely in early automobiles, including the Ford Model T. While most automakers eventually switched to front independent suspension systems, or at least leaf springs that ran parallel with the wheels rather than the axle, Ford cars continued to use transverse leaf springs at Henry Ford's insistence.

The heavy Lincoln-Zephyr, which had a wheelbase that was 10 inches longer than

transverse leaf springs, creating a pendulum effect as the car tended to rock from side to side due to wind, turning, or road conditions. When a new steering system was introduced in the Fords in 1934, the swaying motion affected steering. As Ford engineers worked to offer car buyers a softer, controlled ride, ride-stabilizing torsion bars were added to the 1940 Fords, Mercurys, and Zephyrs. These offered noticeable improvements but were still considered inferior to the competing

Two Fords for 1938

When the 1938 Fords debuted, the Standard had a reworked 1937 front end while the De Luxe had an entirely different and larger appearance. The V-8-60 was retained, but the 85-horsepower engine received a midyear upgrade, going from the 21-stud to the 24-stud cylinder head design for better sealing and performance at lower speeds. The 24-stud design entered production in December 1937, but the Rouge Motor Building continued building the 1937 V-8-85 21-stud engines for service replacement and industrial use until October 1938.

Initially the Standard was so plain looking that most buyers shied away from it. De Luxe sales outpaced the Standard by 20 to 1. Ford added horizontal chrome strips that helped boost the Standard's sales. Many (but not all) cars in dealer stock and storage were retro-fitted with this "brightwork."

The Standard with the V-8-60 had a starting price of $595 for the Coupe and up to $710 for the Fordor Sedan. Standard cars were equipped with front and rear bumpers and guards, spare wheel and tire and tube, tire lock and band, one taillight, one windshield wiper, one sun visor, a cigar lighter, and twin electric horns.

The 1938 De Luxe V-8 was available in eight body styles—Coupe, Club Coupe, Tudor and Fordor sedans, Convertible Cabriolet, Club Convertible Cabriolet, Convertible Sedan (Tudor and Fordor models), and the Phaeton—with the V-8-85 and were priced from $685 for the Coupe to $900 for the Convertible Sedan. Ford had reduced the number of body styles offered, eliminating the Roadsters.

The $820 Phaeton, one of the most expensive cars in the Ford lineup, was offered for the last time, but the Station Wagon became a bona fide passenger car offered as a De Luxe model. Ford sold 6,000 wagons that year, a significant sales jump that made competing manufacturers take notice. For the 1939 through 1941 model years, the wagon was available in both the Standard and De Luxe lines.

Along with the equipment found on the Ford Standard, the De Luxe had twin taillights, dual wipers and dual visors, a deluxe steering wheel, cigar lighter, glove compartment with a recessed clock and lock, chrome wheel bands, a headlight indicator, and more luggage space.

The modernized Ford showroom at 1710 Broadway, New York City, was where Ford held its own exhibit to run concurrently with the New York Auto Show in October 1937. The new 1938 Ford V-8s are on display. At the far right, a V-8 chassis revolves vertically. The sepia photo mural, the largest of its kind ever made up to that time, shows a research engineer, manufacturing scenes, and assembly and transportation systems. Fifteen thousand people visited the showroom during its first day. *National Automotive History Collection, Detroit Public Library*

A man picks up mail in a 1938 Ford Standard Tudor Sedan. From the 1938 to 1940 model years, the Standard and De Luxe Ford cars had distinctive front ends. The 1938 Standard had a reworked 1937 grille, while the De Luxe had a larger appearance. *The Henry Ford*

Flowing Lines

Larger in appearance, the De Luxe had a longer hood than the Standard with a nearly vertical front end featuring a "V" carried down into the radiator grille and the familiar V-8 emblem at the tip of the "V." The horizontal lines of the grille bar and the louvers were echoed in a bright rustless steel band carried along the belt to the rear.

Efforts were made to correct the 1937 Fordor Sedan's stubby look by reworking the body sheet metal behind the rear door, providing a long flowing curve from the roofline to the rear bumper. The car looked heavier at the back, but the shape was left unaltered through the 1940 model. Fenders in both the Standard and De Luxe cars were massive and provided more complete coverage of the running gear and extended farther back. Headlamps were again recessed in front fender aprons,

while new teardrop taillamps were molded to conform to both the rear vertical line and the transverse contour. Safety glass was used for the Ford's windshield, doors, and rear window, and Ford was the only automaker to still offer a hinged ventilating windshield in 1938.

The luggage compartment in all cars was closed off from the passenger space by a wall and locked with a separate key, while the rear handle was in the shape of an airplane propeller and hub with the oval Ford logo. The spare wheel and tire were stored in the trunk, except in the Convertible Cabriolet, where it was mounted behind the rumble seat.

Interior Details

Ford interior colors and textures followed popular late-1930s clothing and furniture fashions, using mahogany, stained birch,

Right: A new year meant a new front end for the 1938 Ford De Luxe V-8, which came in eight body styles, including the Sedan shown here. The V-8-85 was standard on all De Luxe models. *The Henry Ford*

Below: A 1938 Ford V-8 De Luxe Phaeton convertible and a Convertible Club Coupe are parked in front of Michigan's Botsford Tavern. A declining number of buyers wanted open-aired cars and both these body styles would disappear from Ford's lineup in 1939. *The Henry Ford*

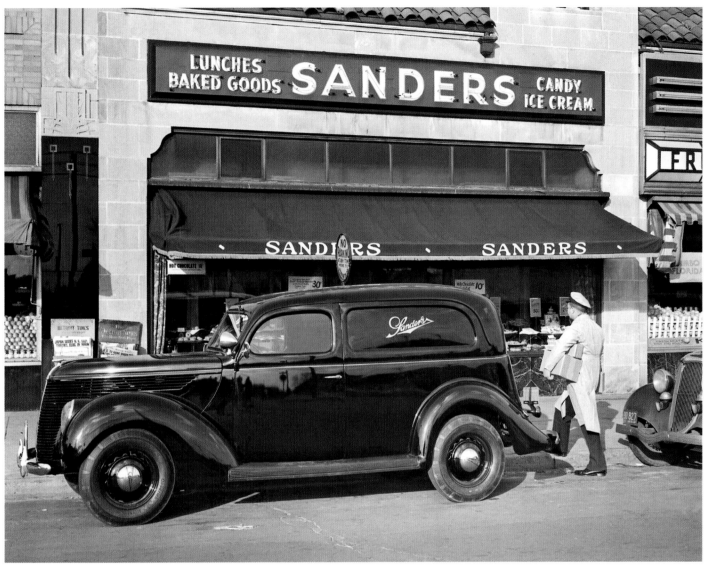

This 1938 Ford Standard Sedan Delivery was owned by the Sanders Company in Detroit. The Sedan Delivery and Station Wagons had a front end similar to the 1938 Standard Ford. An optional De Luxe package could be ordered along with a passenger seat and sliding rear window. The spare tire could be mounted inside or on the rear door. *The Henry Ford*

and other medium to dark woods, while upholstery colors were taupes, tans, and grays with accents in chrome, brown, ivory, or tan plastic. The De Luxe instrument panel had a walnut-grain finish, while the Standard had a mahogany finish, with the gauges arranged in two groups directly in front of the driver. The middle of the panel had a grille where an optional radio could be installed, and the glove compartment was at the right.

The instrument panel design was created by Sheldrick in one day after Sorensen realized in March 1937 that one hadn't been designed for the 1938 models.

For night-driving, the headlamp beam was activated by a toe-operated button on the floor while a light on the instrument panel indicated whether the lights were in the low- or high-beam position. Interior lights were located on the right and left pillars of the sedans and over the rear windows of coupes.

Both front and rear seats were wide enough for three people, and the seat cushions and backs were finished in piping and a pillow treatment.

In the Standard, mohair and broadcloth were optional in cars equipped with the V-8-85, and mohair was only available as a special order item for the "60" cars. The De Luxe had interior options, including light taupe mohair or broadcloth for closed cars, tan hand-buffed antique finish leather or taupe Bedford cord for the convertibles, and tan leather in the Phaeton. The seat cushion and back of the rumble seat in the Convertible Cabriolet were finished in artificial leather.

The driver's seats in all cars except the Phaeton were adjustable, while the full-width front seats of the Tudor Sedans had divided seatbacks and were hinged diagonally so as to swing inward as they were tipped forward. This provided a wide passageway on either side for passengers to get into the backseat.

New Style for Commercial Cars, Trucks

Ford's commercial cars and trucks were also restyled for 1938, and for the first time in the automaker's 35-year history, it offered its most diversified lineup with four wheelbase options. The 112-inch-wheelbase commercial cars, based on the Ford car chassis, could be outfitted with stake, panel, Sedan Delivery, pickup, or Station Wagon bodies, or as a cab and chassis. The Sedan Delivery and Station Wagons had a front end similar to the 1938 Standard Ford, while the stake, panel, and pickup trucks had a vertical oval grille, similar to that found on the larger commercial trucks.

The truck grille gave the front end a more massive, impressive appearance and was highlighted by long louvers extending horizontally along the sides of the hood. Inside, the trucks and commercial cars were fully lined with embossed veal grain "art leather" in two-tone green; the seat cushions and backs were covered with the same material. The cab doors had improved sealing against the outside weather.

Ford trucks were available in the 122-, 134- (which replaced the 131 1/2-inch wheelbase chassis), and 157-inch wheelbases, plus a 191-inch wheelbase bus chassis. The new "one-tonner" truck

had a 122-inch wheelbase and was designed to permit the wider use of the 60-horsepower engine. It was available in the panel, express (pickup-style), stake, and platform body styles, as well as a chassis and cab. For the first time, the automaker offered a new two-speed rear axle as standard equipment. Controlled by the driver shifting a lever, the transmission's high gear was for operating efficiently at highway speeds with the axle operated as a conventional one-speed axle with the driveshaft pinion making 5.83 revolutions to 1 revolution of the wheels. The low gear ratio was for low-speed pulling power and fast acceleration from a dead stop with a ratio change of 37.3 revolutions to 1.

In May 1938, Ford introduced a new cab-over-engine (COE) truck for its 101- and 134-inch wheelbase trucks that were powered by the V-8-85. This design gave the 101-inch COE chassis the same cargo space as a conventional 134-inch truck chassis, while the 134-inch COE was the same as the conventional 157-inch chassis.

Depression Returns

As the 1938 models were shown, used car sales slowed in late 1937 as banks tightened credit terms, dealers reported a jittery

Ford's first cab-over-engine (COE) tractor-trailer combinations were introduced in 1938. Available in 101- and 134-inch-wheelbase units, they were especially useful to truckers in states that had overall truck length limits. *The Henry Ford*

A worker adjusts the brakes on a 1938 Ford Standard Fordor Sedan at the Rouge. Because it was near impossible to route the mechanical brake rods through the chassis of the more complex car, the 1938 models had improved cable-controlled brakes, but the public still thought this was an antiquated feature. *The Henry Ford*

feeling in the economy. *Automobile Topics* noted: "Even those who are working steadily, as well as local merchants, are not inclined to buy unless they have to." The used car problem began damming up the normal stream of new car business because dealers were unable to keep used stocks moving. It was a sign of the economy falling back into a depression. Buyers shied away

from Ford showrooms, making 1938 the worst year for Ford sales since 1933—its domestic sales were a paltry 363,688 units with total sales of 410,048 vehicles worldwide. Of course it was a tough year on the entire industry, as car sales plunged by nearly half from 3.4 million units in 1937 to 1.89 million for 1938. Car sales would not return to 1937 levels until 1950.

Chapter Three

Design Prevails

As the automotive industry unleashed its 1938 models on the roads in the fall of 1937, four years of recovery ground to a halt and reversed itself. Industrial production nose-dived by 37 percent, returning to 1934 levels. Unemployment spiked upward from 14.3 percent in 1937 to 19 percent in early 1938; 12 million people were out of work.

The causes of the so-called "Roosevelt Recession" are still debated by economists. Some condemned stifling New Deal policies, taxes, sit-down strikes, and tight bank lending policies. New Dealers blamed an unequal distribution of wealth, large corporations for monopolizing investment, and the richest 1 percent of Americans for having more income than the bottom third of the nation. By January 1938, 320,000 autoworkers were furloughed while another 196,000 were placed on short work weeks. In Detroit, about 200,000 of the UAW's 250,000 members were laid off as the city's unemployment rate climbed to 41 percent. The union's promises of better working conditions seemed empty.

Fortune magazine indicted the auto industry, saying, "Just as Detroit's generally low-price, big-volume philosophy has more than once led us out of a depression, so the abrupt surrender of its production to a falling demand hurries us into them; Detroit is probably the birthplace of both good times and bad times."

The automakers couldn't afford to ignore market forces. When sales of used cars slowed, it depressed new car sales. Jack Davis, Ford's general sales manager, determined that an industrywide effort was needed to break the sales logjam. He asked Edsel Ford to present a plan to the Automotive Manufacturers Association, the industry's chamber of commerce.

"They won't listen to you," Edsel replied, knowing his father's dislike for the organization.

"Maybe not, but may I talk with them?" Davis rejoined. Edsel agreed.

The Danger of Used Cars

"The Danger of Used Cars" and similar headlines occasionally appeared in Depression-era automotive trade journals. The secondary market was an important part of the industry—for every new car purchase, there was usually a used car with residual value to trade in. Because no two used cars were alike, there was a lot of haggling between dealers and buyers. And dealers continually financed the cars they had in stock; the longer a car sat unsold, the more it ate into profits. In early 1938, the stock of used cars had swelled to financially dangerous levels.

Talking to Alvin Macauley, president of the AMA and head of Packard, Jack Davis proposed that the industry needed to sell off as many used cars as possible. The result was the first cooperative effort ever undertaken by all the American automakers. Edsel, GM's Bill Knudsen, and Chrysler's K. T. Keller even met with President Roosevelt in January to receive his approval.

The scheme to pull the country out of the recession and stimulate business growth was announced in New York on February 27, 1938. Macauley, speaking on behalf of the automakers and the nation's 46,000 dealers, declared that "National Used Car Exchange Week" would be held March 5 to 12. It was an all-out effort to sell or scrap as many old cars as possible, especially the 11 million or so obsolete old cars (nearly half of the estimated 22 million used cars, many of which were Model Ts and As) that didn't have "modern equipment." The automakers spent a combined $1.25 million to promote the event. Among the activities surrounding National Used Car Exchange Week were funeral pyres of old automobiles, parades of used cars, and economy runs (long-distance driving demonstrations), while proclamations of support came from mayors and civic organizations nationwide.

To keep track of company sales, Davis arranged for daily telegraphic returns from Ford dealers. Ford led the industry by selling more than 57,000 vehicles during the week and trimmed its used car stocks by 22,804 units. The promotion was not a panacea, but it helped the industry at a time when it was grasping for good news.

Facing: A 1939 Ford De Luxe Station Wagon is loaded with produce at Valerie Jean's Date Shop on Route 66 in the Coachella Valley, California, on March 28, 1939. Although still advertised with Ford's commercial vehicles, the Station Wagon was now touted for its passenger-hauling capabilities and interior refinements. The 1939 Station Wagon came in De Luxe and Standard versions, sharing many of the features of the passenger cars, including the grilles. Other exterior improvements included chrome-plating for the carriage bolts and other visible hardware. *The Henry Ford*

When there wasn't a spring upturn in the economy, President Roosevelt sent a $3 billion public works and relief bill to Congress. He blamed the recession on corporate executive officers who "can't see further than the next dividend." Since the car companies tended to oppose him, Roosevelt unleashed the antitrust investigators against the Big Three. The Department of Justice indicted Ford, General Motors, and Chrysler for favoring specific finance companies. The dispute with the government was later resolved with Ford and Chrysler signing consent decrees promising not to advertise particular finance companies for handling installment sales. GM refused to accept the agreement if it meant losing General Motors Acceptance Corporation (GMAC), so other arrangements were made.

Other trouble was brewing for the Ford Motor Company in the form of a birthday present.

Henry Ford and the Jews

On July 30, 1938, Henry Ford turned 75, and the Motor City held a three-day celebration that climaxed with a dinner at Detroit's Masonic Temple with more than 1,600 guests, including most of Detroit's automotive elites.

Admirers worldwide—including Adolph Hitler—sent birthday wishes. Germany's Detroit Consul Fritz Hailer and Cleveland Consul Karl Kapp publicly presented Henry with the Grand Cross of the Supreme Order of the German Eagle, the highest Nazi award for a non-German. Henry had the dubious distinction of being the first of two Americans to receive the medal (aviator Charles Lindbergh was the second). At the dinner at the Masonic Temple, Kapp read the fuhrer's citation congratulating Henry for making the automobile available to the masses, an idea that Hitler copied with the founding of Volkswagen ("the people's car").

Two weeks later, as if to punctuate the real reason for honoring Henry, Hitler awarded Ford's personal secretary Ernest Liebold the Third Reich's second highest medal, the First Order of the German Eagle. Liebold was the former president of the *Dearborn Independent*, Henry's personal newspaper in the 1920s that published a long series of anti-Semitic articles based on a discredited work called the *Protocols of the Learned Elders of Zion*.

Published in 1903, the *Protocols* were a hoax, plagiarizing the plot from a satirical French novel as the basis for a pogrom against Jews in tsarist Russia. Yet, in the aftermath of World War I, when people looked to affix blame for the conflict on bankers and war profiteers, Henry accepted the book's

In an effort to sell or scrap as many used cars as possible, America's automotive manufacturers and the 46,000 dealers held National Used Car Exchange Week March 5–12, 1938. Among the event's activities were funeral pyres of old automobiles, parades, and economy runs (long-distance driving demonstrations). Many mayors and civic organizations issued proclamations of support. *The Henry Ford*

Henry Ford sits with General Motors President (and former Ford executive) William S. Knudsen during Henry's 75th birthday party at Detroit's Masonic Temple on July 30, 1938. More than 1,600 guests attended the party, including Chrysler President K. T. Keller and the nationally known poet Edgar Guest. *Walter P. Reuther Library, Wayne State University*

outlandish claim that Jewish conspirators were planning to take over nations and companies.

Henry believed that the so-called "international Jews"—a term his paper coined—were responsible for starting and perpetuating World War I. While Henry Ford never advocated violence or showed personal animosity toward Jews, his actions inflamed racists from the Ku Klux Klan to the Nazis and other anti-Semites.

Henry Ford's acceptance of the Nazi medal became a lightning rod for criticism from Jewish groups and the UAW. "The upshot was that Ford products were shunned by Jews in the most complete boycott of automotive vehicles by any group in American history," noted automotive historian and retired University of Michigan Professor David L. Lewis. "Jews virtually stopped buying Ford products, and some of their Gentile sympathizers did the same. This boycott was to cost the Ford Company tens of millions of dollars in lost sales."

A Martyr's Smile

Soon after his birthday, Henry suffered his first stroke. The incident was hushed as the feisty auto pioneer pursued an aggressive recovery regime, countermanding advice from Henry Ford Hospital doctors. Within a month he returned to his activities but at a diminished capacity. Instead of turning the company's reins over to his son, Henry relied more and more

Help Americanize Ford

Why did Ford receive the highest Nazi decoration?

Why did Ford employ Fritz Kuhn, <u>Convicted</u> Bund Leader?

Why did Ford refuse to build plane motors for England?

Why has Ford refused to abide by the laws of the U. S. A.?

BE AMERICAN: BUY UNION-MADE CARS

Ford, Only Non-union Car Made in America

FORD COMMITTEE
UNITED AUTOMOBILE WORKERS

This union-organizing leaflet distributed in 1940 criticized Henry Ford for accepting a medal from the Nazi government, for flouting Roosevelt's pro-labor policies, and for refusing to build military aircraft engines for England. Fritz Kuhn, a German-born, naturalized American citizen, was a chemist who briefly worked for Ford Hospital in the 1930s and led the German-American Bund, a group connected to Adolf Hitler and the Nazi Party. *Walter P. Reuther Library, Wayne State University*

on Bennett, ratcheting up efforts to "toughen" Edsel through various humiliations and slights.

Bennett had almost unrestricted authority; he could even alter company policies by saying that Mr. Ford wanted it done. Mead Bricker, production aide to Charles Sorensen, said, "Often we suspected that he wasn't speaking for Mr. Ford, but we couldn't check on it."

"[Bennett] had to approve all travel vouchers," recounted Laurence Sheldrick, chief engineer. "One could not hire, fire, raise, or transfer a man [without Bennett knowing of it and confirming it]. I could not send a man on a trip; I could not make a long-distance phone call; I could not send a telegram if he didn't want me to."

Edsel maintained a "martyr's smile" as his orders were countermanded or altered, or when Bennett fired trusted employees. Seemingly acquiescing at first when his father made a decision, Edsel often said, "If that's the way father wants it, that's the way it's going to be." Yet the tragedy seemed to be that Henry wanted Edsel to stand up and fight more for his ideas.

One of Bennett's methods to increase his power was to put other Ford executives into his debt and then pressure them to appoint people who were loyal to him or to use friendly contractors. Or if he wanted to discredit someone, such as Edsel, he would watch their actions and then haphazardly mention the damning information to Henry.

Frustrated, Edsel once revealed to a friend, "The hurtful thing is that Father takes Harry's word for everything and won't believe me. Who is this guy? Where did he come from?"

Simultaneous with Henry's declining health, Edsel got colds easily and had increasingly serious stomach problems. Numerous sources have related details of Edsel's ailments, including Peter Collier's and David Horowitz's *The Fords: An American Epic*, as well as Ford Bryan's *Henry's Lieutenants*. The doctors at Henry Ford Hospital informed Edsel that he had ulcers and placed him on a strict diet, but his "gastritis" was a portent of the stomach cancer he developed in the early 1940s.

Henry's wife, Clara, once confronted Sorensen about Bennett's relationship with Henry. Crying, she asked, "Who is

Mayer Smither of Tacoma, Washington, and his wife take delivery of their new 1938 Ford Standard Coupe at Mallon Motors Company. The Standard was so plain looking that many buyers shied away from it and the De Luxe outsold it by a 20 to 1 margin. Ford quickly added horizontal chrome strips that helped boost the Standard's sales. Many (but not all) cars in dealer stock and storage were retrofitted with the "brightwork" molding. *The Henry Ford*

It's not exactly cruising weather, but Depression-era Ford public relations pictures were taken where and when they could be, such as wintertime in Michigan. The driver of this car—which has a rear seat—has two women and a male passenger crammed next to him. The title of this photo was "What Not to Do While Driving a 1938 Ford V-8 Tudor De Luxe Convertible Coupe." *The Henry Ford*

this man Bennett who has so much control over my husband and is ruining my son's health?" By this point, Sorensen was nearly powerless to stop Henry's "little man" (a derogatory nickname some people used to describe Bennett). "I couldn't answer the question," Sorensen recounted. "I couldn't tell her that Bennett did not control Henry Ford but that the reverse was true."

As he later recalled in his autobiography, when Bennett had taken over as head of the Ford Service Department, he heard that his predecessor was fired for refusing to do what Henry had asked. Bennett swore to do whatever Henry commanded. In answering a reporter's question on that subject, while Henry stood by, Bennett replied, "If Mr. Ford told me to blacken out the sun tomorrow, I might have trouble fixing it. But you'd see a hundred thousand sons-of-bitches coming through the Rouge gates in the morning, all wearing dark glasses."

One of the things Henry wanted was to keep the UAW out of his factories, and Bennett—who in 1936 had worked his way into the good graces of UAW President Homer Martin—did everything in his power to try to fulfill his wish. (He also disrupted Ku Klux Klan efforts to organize white workers in the factories.) Service Department men followed workers into washrooms to find out what they were discussing; lunch pails and overcoats were searched for union materials while workers were on the line.

Outside the plant, more spies listened in bars and markets (some of the spy reports still exist in the files at the Benson Ford Research Center). Bennett's operatives tear-gassed union meetings. Between 1937 and 1941, more than 4,000 Ford workers were fired for union activities, and many of these workers allegedly were beaten.

The union fought back in various ways. The Reuther brothers once rented a plane with speakers and buzzed the Rouge, though

This collage shows the multiple assembly operations used to make the 1938 Ford, including a white-hot 10-ton steel ingot being transferred from a soaking pit to a buggy for further processing, the engine-boring and steel-stamping processes, the body drop, engine testing, welding, and chassis assembly. *The Henry Ford*

This 1938 Tudor Sedan is one of eight body styles offered that year for the De Luxe V-8 line. The 85-horsepower engine received a midyear upgrade, going from the 21-stud to the 24-stud cylinder head design for better sealing and performance at lower speeds. *The Henry Ford*

the noise of the engine drowned out much of their message. Dearborn outlawed demonstrations around the Rouge until a court decision overturned the law in 1940, after which some union organizers went on public plant tours and flashed labor buttons to the workers. In the meantime the UAW-CIO used a low-watt radio station in Detroit to broadcast its messages to sympathizers.

Edsel believed that the industry should seek accommodation with the union before violence broke out in the factories, but his father regarded such notions as another sign of his son's weakness. Eventually that accommodation would be forced on Ford during the 1941 strike.

Atmosphere of Experimentation

Edsel's refuge was the Ford Design Department. After the executive round table luncheons, he walked down the Engineering Laboratory's central corridor and went into Gregorie's office. Sometimes they sat and talked in one of the prototype models or made decisions at the end of a drafting table rather than in a staff meeting.

"He came in practically every day," said draftsman Joe Galamb. "Edsel liked to criticize the first model made in clay. He [might not] like the shape of the grille, the back end, and so on. He criticized the interior quite a lot and the instrumental work. . . . He was very particular about the riding qualities of the car. He knew what he wanted and insisted that he get it."

Gregorie was one of the few people in the company that Edsel could talk to without fear of betrayal, though he kept many matters private. "After meetings Edsel had with his

This editorial cartoon says it all. Even as the new models were hitting dealer showrooms in the fall of 1937, four years of economic recovery ground to a halt. Industrial production nose-dived by 37 percent, returning to 1934 levels. *The Henry Ford*

father … it would take him a half-hour or more to get his reasoning back," Gregorie said. "It was this constant wrangling with the old man that eventually wore Edsel down. It eventually killed him."

Unlike the dictatorial supervision in the factories, Gregorie was generally supportive of his staff's ideas. He also introduced an important innovation to the automotive industry. Resembling an upside-down U, styling bridges rode on a series of parallel rails and originated in the shipbuilding industry to design hulls from small models using a table of offsets. Under Gregorie's guidance, a series of aluminum styling bridges were built at the Rouge; the devices could precisely determine the coordinates on any clay model at 1/10-inch intervals on a three-dimensional axis, pinpoint hardpoint locations (for the engine, axles, and so on), and replicate the design from one side of a clay model to the other. These styling bridges were used to create the 1938 Fords.

A 1938 Sedan body receives touch-up paint before it's mated to the chassis. *The Henry Ford*

Technological improvements marched on despite the Depression and labor unrest. This is a freshly painted 1938 Ford V-8 body traveling through the new infrared drying oven at the Rouge. The oven clamped around the car and moved with it down the line for several minutes. The lamps generated temperatures in the range of 300 to 325 degrees Fahrenheit, baking on the finish in a few minutes. *The Henry Ford*

Ford's Village Industries

When Henry Ford created the Rouge Plant as a masterpiece of vertical integration—a vast factory complex capable of taking raw materials and turning them into finished cars—he concurrently started the Village Industries that dispersed the production of various vehicle components and tools. Located in small-town factories, many of which were dilapidated grist or sawmills before Ford resurrected them, the plants employed people who supplemented their factory employment with farm work.

By the late 1930s, upward of 2,500 people were employed in the Village Industries, located on the upper reaches of the Rouge, Huron, and Raisin rivers, all in southeastern Michigan and mostly within 50 miles of Dearborn. These small plants made parts for V-8s, Mercurys, and Lincoln-Zephyrs. Village Industries factories were hydroelectrically powered, though some were supplemented with energy from the power grid or electrical generators powered by V-8 motors.

The first Village Industry opened in 1920 with 35 men who made engine valves in an 1896-era woodworking plant in Northville. In December 1936, that plant was replaced with a new Albert Kahn–designed brick-and-steel structure that was about one-third bigger than the old mill. On a landscaped setting complete with a water-powered overshot wheel, the Northville plant was air conditioned and employed 300 people who did finishing work on 70,000 engine valves a day. Rough valve castings were poured at the Rouge foundry and shipped to Northville for grinding, final machining, and inspection.

The second Village Industry was Nankin Mills, an old flour mill in Westland that made the dies that produced the Ford script on almost every part of the Ford V-8, the Lincoln-Zephyr, and the Lincoln motor car, plus the dies to make Ford factory identification badges, stencils, and other engravings. The Ypsilanti plant, which opened in 1932 along the Huron River, was the largest, employing 850 men who assembled generators, starters, and starter switches used in Ford V-8 and Zephyr cars. The second largest plant was in Flat Rock, employing 460 people who made headlamps, taillamps, and dome lamps.

The 1845-era Schuyler gristmill in Saline (near Ann Arbor) was renovated and opened in 1938 to process soybeans grown at the Ford Farms and by other farmers within a 200-mile radius. After a 1937 tornado tore through the swampy area just north of Brooklyn—situated in the Irish Hills, now home to the Michigan International Speedway—Henry Ford built a new plant where the tangle of storm-swept woods was the thickest. Completed in summer 1938, the plant produced about 1,500 Ford horns a day.

Some of the other Village Industries were the Phoenix Mill (Plymouth Township), where 50 to 150 women assembled generators, generator cutouts, voltage regulators, and stop-light switches; the Plymouth plant where 33 men made taps; the Waterford Mill that produced high-precision gauges used by Ford inspectors; the Newburgh plant where twist drills were made; the Cherry Hill (Canton Township) plant that employed disabled World War I veterans; and the Dundee plant that opened in 1937 to make electrodes used in Ford factories.

In addition, Henry had the 1835-era Hayden Mill in Tecumseh restored for use of cleaning and sacking soybeans for seed. The Manchester plant produced ammeters, charge indicators, instrument clusters, and oil, temperature, and fuel gauges. The Milan plant opened in 1939 to process soybeans for industrial use while workers encased ignition coils in soybean plastic. The Milford plant manufactured Ford V-8 carburetors, and Sharon Hallow, another former gristmill, opened in 1939 to make Ford instrument panels.

Many of these plants did not make money and, in some cases, were underpowered. After World War II, when Ford Motor Company faced a severe financial crisis, Henry Ford II ordered most of them closed and sold off.

When Henry Ford created the Rouge plant as a masterpiece of vertical integration—a vast factory complex capable of turning raw materials into finished cars—he concurrently started the Village Industries that dispersed the production of various vehicle components and tools. Shown here are Nankin Mills (where nuts, bolts, and small stampings were made), Flat Rock (headlamps and taillights), Phoenix Mill (generator cutouts), Waterford (gauges), the dam for Plymouth's hydroelectric power plant, Plymouth (engine taps), Ypsilanti (generators and starter motors), the interior of Rawsonville's hydroelectric plant, and the first Northville plant (engine valves). *The Henry Ford*

Riding on a 112-inch wheelbase, the 1938 De Luxe V-8 Panel Delivery had a vertical oval grille similar to that found on the larger commercial trucks. Also unlike the V-8 passenger cars, the headlights were mounted in pods rather than on the fenders. The cargo space could be lined with wood slats or Masonite. The following year, the truck was available only as a Standard model, though Ford offered it on the 122-inch "one-tonner" and the 134-inch wheelbase chassis. *The Henry Ford*

Gregorie and his assistant, Ed Martin, prepared charts comparing Ford's cars and prices versus those offered by GM and Chrysler and proposed new models. By mid-1937, the Design Department took over styling all of Ford's vehicles, and by 1939 was working on redesigns of the entire lineup.

Styling decisions came quickly, noted Bob Thomas, who was a design apprentice in the late 1930s. After showing a rear deck handle sketch to Gregorie, Thomas said, "He told me to draw it up and have it made at the Rouge Plant. About two weeks later, this beautiful chrome-plated model appeared in the studio. The thing was cast in solid brass. . . . When the time came to choose a rear deck handle . . . Edsel Ford came into the studio after lunch in the lab. I remember waiting breathlessly as he picked up my design and said, 'This is it.'"

Despite Edsel's protection, the department was not entirely immune to executive power plays. Henry instructed Bennett and Sheldrick to spy on Gregorie's operation. Holes were drilled in the partitions between the Styling and Engineering departments while gate watchmen kept track of Gregorie, looking for a way to fire him.

With a late-season sales surge toward the end of August 1938, Ford briefly resumed production of the 1938 models. About 24,000 workers were recalled to the Rouge and some branch assembly plants even as Ford prepared to unveil the 1939 models, which had new grilles, thanks to an innovation on the Lincoln-Zephyr.

A New Face for Automobiles

The Lincoln-Zephyr had been completely restyled for 1938 with four more body styles and a longer wheelbase. But most significant was its new radically styled front end. Instead of a conventional vertical grille, it had two horizontal rectangular openings near the bottom. Although Gordon Buehrig's 1936 Cord 810 had preceded the Zephyr with a horizontal grille, many designers have noted that the Zephyr set the horizontal grille trend. In fact, when General Motors' Harley Earl saw a picture of the '38 Zephyr, he remarked, "My God, how did we miss on that one? That's going to ruin us."

The location and size of the openings was determined not for styling purpose but as a practical solution to the

Zephyr's overheating problems. Coming back from lunch one day, Gregorie stood in front of a Zephyr chassis. He looked at its skinny, tall radiator core that mostly sat well above the car's crank-mounted fan. The fan's position was the result of a Henry Ford requirement for the V-8 that carried over to the Zephyr's V-12.

Determining that the radiator could be turned crossways to fit between the side rails, Gregorie sketched a new design that placed the radiator core down in front of the fan.

"Edsel Ford came in that afternoon, and I told him what we were doing there," Gregorie said. "He said, 'Well … maybe we *can* cool this thing.'"

After Gregorie's team whipped together a rough sheet-metal front end, a prototype Zephyr was tested in Ford's new wind tunnel. In tests from normal to boiling temperatures under a full load, the radiator cooled fine. With Edsel's approval,

Gregorie created the new grille for the car. Since the Fords also suffered from overheating problems, the same fix was given to the 1939 De Luxe. Problem solved.

The Zephyr's horizontal grille carried over into the 1939 Ford and Mercury, but it was also later copied by Packard, Buick, and others; vertical grilles all but disappeared on most future models.

Filling the Gap: The Mercury Eight

The 1939 Mercury Eight competed in the medium-priced field—the $775 to $925 price range—filling the gap between the De Luxe Ford and the Lincoln-Zephyr. Until the 1937 recession, medium-priced cars had been the industry's fastest growing segment; the estimated market size for 1939 was 1 million cars.

In development for more than a year, the Mercury made the biggest news splash even though the revamped Zephyr and

Steel hubcaps are dipped into a chemical vat to help rustproof them during the chrome-plating process in March 1938. *The Henry Ford*

65

the 1939 Fords were revealed simultaneously. Using a modified, longer Ford chassis reinforced with an X-member, the Mercury had a 116-inch wheelbase and was 4 inches longer than the Ford but 6 inches shorter than the Zephyr, so it also filled a size gap between Ford's car lines.

It was powered by a 239-cubic-inch V-8 that was adapted from the V-8-85, and it produced an advertised 95 horsepower at 3,600 rpm. The car's cruising speed was about 60 miles per hour. Although the speedometer went up to 100, the top speed was about 90 miles per hour.

Significantly, the Mercury—and most of the Ford lineup—was equipped with hydraulic brakes, answering dealers' longtime demands. Only the Lincoln K, which would be phased out after 1940, retained mechanical brakes.

On the exterior, the Mercury shared the "family" appearance of the Fords and the Lincoln-Zephyr with the low horizontal grille and the inverted boat bow–shaped hood. The cars also had more headroom than competitors' models because,

as Henry Ford required, any farmers who bought them could wear their hats while driving.

The Mercury had high crowned front fenders with flush-mounted headlights, while the shallow valley between the fenders and the hood produced a more unified appearance. It had rounded body contours while the rear fender sides dropped to below tire level, partially enclosing the rear wheels (a design difference from the Fords).

The 18-inch-diameter, two-spoke steering wheel was 1 inch larger than the Ford and set closer to the dash, giving the driver increased leverage for the manual steering and a little more passenger room. The instrument panel grouped all the gauges in front of the driver, control buttons were recessed, and it had a die-cast radio grille. The seats were wide and deep.

The Mercury was available in five body styles, including the two-door Sedan, the Town Sedan, Sedan-Coupe, and Sport Convertible with prices ranging from $920 to $1,180. The standard Ford and the Ford De Luxe ranged from $540 to $920,

In this 1939 photo of the Ford Design Department inside the Engineering Laboratory Building, Bob Thomas, future designer of the 1956 and 1961 Lincoln Continentals, works on a design buck at the far left. A 1940 Ford De Luxe Fordor Sedan is in the foreground under a styling bridge where designer Emmett O'Rear, wearing a vest, is stooped over. To his right is Bruno Kolt, responsible for grilles and exterior trim. The next row back is Ross Cousins, wearing a white smock and showing a rendering to office manager Frank Francis. At a drafting table in the far background, wearing a white shirt and dark tie, and leaning over is Martin Regitko, responsible for body layout and engineering. *Garnet Cousins archives*

A young family with a new 1939 Mercury four-door Sedan, complete with "suicide" doors, is pictured in a publicity shot taken in 1938 with American Airlines' flagship DC-3, named *The Mercury*. National Automotive History Collection, Detroit Public Library

while the Zephyr started at $1,360. "This car has been brought out to expand, not to divide, the business which belongs to Ford and Lincoln-Zephyr," Jack Davis told Ford dealers.

Reducing Variation

The Ford brand's two cars for 1939 were the V-8 and the De Luxe V-8. The name "Standard" was officially dropped, though early sales literature, newspapers, and dealers still referred to the base model as the Standard up through 1940. (At other times the standard V-8 was referred to as either the 60-horsepower series or the 85-horsepower series to distinguish it from the De Luxe.) The V-8 had a modified 1938 De Luxe heart-shaped grille with slight modifications. The 1939 De Luxe's low-mounted, horizontal grille was styled with vertical bars to match the fenders' contours, while the flush-mounted headlights were moved out to the fenders' crowns.

Under the hood, the De Luxe's 85-horsepower engine was upgraded with a larger crankshaft, 2 1/2-inch main bearings, valve seat inserts on all valves, and new piston rings with steel inner expander rings for greater and more even wall pressure that improved performance and oil economy.

Again, the standard V-8 (the Model 922A) had the "thrifty sixty" engine but could be ordered with the V-8-85. As noted, for the first time all Ford cars were equipped with hydraulic brakes. The all-welded steel bodies, basically unchanged from the previous year, used new insulating materials to reduce road noise.

Due to the poor economy, Ford trimmed the number of body style and color options. The De Luxe was available in seven colors, but the body styles dropped from eight to five and that included the Tudor and Fordor Sedans, the Coupe, Convertible Coupe, and Convertible Sedan. The Phaeton, which only sold 1,169 units the previous model year, was gone from the lineup along with Club Coupe and Club Convertible.

The Convertible Coupe featured the last year for the Ford rumble seat. The De Luxe Convertible Sedan had a normal sedan trunk, but a larger canvas top than previous models.

Standard V-8 customers had three color and three body style choices: the Tudor and Fordor Sedans and the Coupe. The Coupe was capable of carrying three passengers in the single bench seat; it was a tight fit, especially with the gearshift in the middle of the floor. The dashboard was similar to that of the 1938 cars, but it had an angular theme, with no curves except for the dials.

The Ford V-8s faced tough competition in the lower end of the market. Chevrolet fielded a new car with many mechanical innovations, including a front wishbone-type, coil-spring independent suspension plus new rear shocks and an improved 85-horsepower six-cylinder engine for the Chevy Master De Luxe.

Woodies for Passengers, Utility

Although still advertised with its commercial vehicles, Ford began touting its Station Wagon's passenger-hauling

A 1938 Lincoln K and a Lincoln-Zephyr are near the end of the final assembly line at the Lincoln plant in Detroit. The Zephyr in particular shows the changing face of automobiles with its two horizontal grille openings as opposed to the K's vertical grille. The Zephyr's new grille and radiator placement corrected the car's overheating problem by moving both closer to the crank-mounted cooling fan. The 1939 and 1940 Ford and Mercury models adopted the Zephyr's leading-edge look. *The Henry Ford*

capabilities and interior refinements. The 1939 wagon came in the De Luxe and standard V-8 versions, sharing many of the passenger cars' features, including the grilles. Other exterior improvements included chrome plating for the carriage bolts and other visible hardware.

As passenger vehicles, both wagon versions could comfortably fit eight people. The De Luxe was upholstered in genuine leather. The side windows and all doors except for the front passenger-side door locked from the inside. Only the front passenger door and the tailgate could be opened by a key from the outside. (The doors on all 1938 and 1939 Ford cars had the lock on the passenger door only as a safety measure. At a time when parallel parking dominated cities, by putting the lock on the curb side, the driver was encouraged to enter and exit that way instead of stepping out into traffic. Either version of the Station Wagon could be converted into a utility-hauling vehicle by removing the rear and center seats, though Ford stressed

that the standard wagon was designed for the workaday world where sturdiness and adaptability were the first requisite.

The Ford wagons faced stiffer competition as Chevrolet, Oldsmobile, Plymouth, Pontiac, Hudson, Packard, Studebaker, and Willys offered more car-based station wagons that mixed utility with comfort features.

Growing Truck Line

As the number of Ford passenger body styles shrank, the 1939 Ford truck and commercial vehicle line gave customers a greater selection of capabilities and options, including hydraulic brakes, eight rear-axle ratios, two clutches, five transmissions, various wheel and tire sizes (even dual rear wheels), and more power than ever before. Thirty-four body and chassis types were available in the truck line, and eight were available in the commercial car line. There was also a choice of three engines—in addition to the "thrifty sixty" and V-8-85 (both of which received refinements similar to the passenger car versions), truck owners could get the new 95-horsepower Mercury V-8 that offered 10 percent greater torque than the "85" at 400 fewer rpm.

Ford had built more than 4 million trucks in 21 years, and 1938 was its last major body redesign for the next decade, though the front grille would be modified. Like the passenger cars, trucks took on an even more streamlined look with heavily rounded fenders and soft cab lines.

The commercial car's 112-inch-wheelbase chassis (basically the passenger car chassis) had a wide range of uses and was available with either the 85- or 60-horsepower engines plus three transmissions: the low-reduction three-speed normally used with the V-8-60, a standard three-speed for the "85," or an optional four-speed. There were three rear axle ratios: 4.44:1 for the V-8-60, 3.78:1 for the "85," or 4.11:1 ratio axle. The chassis was available in panel, stake, platform, pickup, or Sedan Delivery bodies, or could come as a drive-away chassis and cab in two different configurations.

The Sedan Delivery commercial car had a hardwood cargo floor protected by steel skid strips and the standard V-8 grille. The pickup truck had the oval-shaped truck grille,

while skid strips were stamped into the heavy-gauge steel of the pickup bed's floor (there was a wooden subfloor under the pickup box). Buyers could purchase dual wheels, heavy-duty tires, and auxiliary springs at an extra cost.

Ford's commercial trucks came in the 122- (either as the new "three-quarter-tonner" or "one-tonner" configurations), 134-, and 157-inch wheelbase chassis. There was also the 191-inch bus chassis. All trucks were available in two cab-and-chassis drive-away configurations for companies that wanted custom bodies. Other popular styles were the panel, express (pickup), stake, and platform bodies. Ford's COE truck line was expanded and could be had on the 101-, 134-, and the 157-inch wheelbase chassis. Prices on Ford's commercial trucks ranged from $570 up to $1,125.

A Union Divided

After great success in organizing GM and Chrysler in 1937, the UAW's gains deteriorated during the "Roosevelt Recession." About 80 percent of all autoworkers were idled. Union dues fell steeply and the UAW laid off organizers and closed branch offices. UAW President Homer Martin found himself at

A wide selection of 1939 Ford models is shown in this photo. The vehicles are arranged on the tarmac outside of a hangar at Ford Airport in Dearborn. In the background is Henry Ford Museum with its iconic reproduction of Philadelphia's Independence Hall. *The Henry Ford*

The new 1939 Ford De Luxe Fordor Sedan drives over an undulating concrete road at Ford's new testing grounds at Ford Airport. Its welded all-steel body was set on rubber cushions and attached to a heavy frame that was reinforced by an X-member. Although it had hydraulic brakes, it still used Ford's trademark (and somewhat antiquated) transverse cantilever springs, along with four hydraulic shock absorbers. *The Henry Ford*

A 1939 Mercury reaches the end of the assembly line at the Rouge in November 1938. The Mercury mostly competed in the medium-priced field—$775 to $925—and faced stiff competition from 10 other four-door sedans that included the Hudson 6, Hupp Skylark, Pontiac De Luxe Six, Oldsmobile 60, and Dodge De Luxe. Additionally, there were 10 cars within $50 of the lower part of the medium segment, and another 10 were within $50 of the upper end of the segment. *The Henry Ford*

This 1939 advertisement for Ford tires shows several operations at the new $5.6 million tire plant at the Rouge, including the shaping of "green tires" before going into curing molds (waffle-like irons) and on to an inspection line. The plant had the capacity to produce 6,000 tires a day. *The Henry Ford*

odds with the more militant members of his executive board, including the Reuther brothers.

Strife grew within the union. The "Progressive" faction led by Martin wanted a centralized, well-disciplined organization. The "Unity" faction, including the Reuthers, wanted a loose federation of autonomous locals. Additionally, between 1937 and 1939, militant workers became increasingly impatient with the negotiated grievance procedures and staged hundreds of unsanctioned strikes to get what they wanted.

These wildcat strikes undermined Martin's authority because contracts put the onus on union leadership to keep its members in line. Martin asserted that Communists had staged the wildcat strikes. By June 1938, the UAW was torn by infighting with bizarre alliances between UAW leaders of different political leanings jockeying to usurp Martin.

The UAW schism caused a major crisis in the Congress of Industrial Organizations.

Martin and Bennett opened secret labor negotiations and by late December 1938 announced that Ford Motor Company and the UAW reached a tentative agreement. When the UAW Executive Committee demanded details of the agreement, Martin suspended 15 of its 24 members, and two months later announced that he wanted the UAW to rejoin the American Federation of Labor. His rivals formed a second faction, choosing former Chrysler worker R. J. Thomas as its president.

As the UAW-AFL and UAW-CIO fought, GM, Chrysler, Briggs, and other companies nullified their union agreements, claiming that they didn't know which faction was legitimate. Only after government-supervised elections were conducted at the auto plants did the UAW-CIO faction come out

A top view of the 1939 Ford De Luxe Sedan's engine compartment shows the V-8-85 that had a larger crankshaft, 2 1/2- inch main bearings, valve seat inserts on all valves, and new piston rings with steel inner expander rings for greater compression and more even wall pressure that improved performance and oil economy. A few late-model 1939 De Luxes were equipped with the 91A-6000 engine that placed the oil pump on the front main bearing cap, an improved oil pan assembly, and a new distributor. Stamped with an "LW" for lightweight on its left front corner, the 91A-6000 block weighed 160 pounds — 24 pounds lighter than the 81A-6000-B engine block. *The Henry Ford*

overwhelmingly victorious, but labor's drive to organize Ford was delayed by more than two years.

Continental Drift

While the Machiavellian intrigues surrounding the Bennett-Martin secret negotiations swirled about, Bob Gregorie and his design staff worked on the final touches for the "Ford for Forty" car that would be the capstone of their pre–World War II achievements. Yet Gregorie was concerned about Lincoln. Although the Zephyr had saved the brand, the Lincoln K was dying, and Edsel, who had returned from a summer tour of Europe, wanted a car with "continental" styling.

One day in November 1938, Edsel and Gregorie talked about creating a sports car—something that would glorify the Ford line—and reminisced about the 1934 Ford Model 40 Special Speedster Gregorie had made. Gregorie realized that such a car could be built on the Zephyr chassis.

The next day he placed a sheet of vellum over the Zephyr's side-view blueprint. Grabbing a yellow crayon pencil, he began sketching. Using the Zephyr's wheelbase and exterior dimensions, he stretched the hood by about 7 inches by moving the passenger compartment and windshield back. Lowering the roofline, he lengthened the fenders and shortened the trunk. The entire design effort took between 30 minutes and an hour.

When Edsel visited the department, Gregorie showed him his sketch and asked, "How do you like this one?"

"Oh boy," Edsel said. "That looks great. That's it! Don't change a line on it. How fast can you have one built?"

Bypassing the normal design steps, only a 20-inch scale model was created before a full-size running prototype was made using a modified 1939 Lincoln-Zephyr sedan. Rebuilt by

hand at the Lincoln plant, the Zephyr's front end remained virtually stock, but every other body panel changed. Workers sectioned 4 inches from the cowl and the doors to give the body a lower profile, the windshield was raked back, and a hand-fabricated hood and fenders replaced the standard versions. Ross Cousins designed the hood ornament using the 1939–1940 New York World's Fair signature sphere and obelisk buildings as inspiration. To smooth out transitions from one body panel to the next, Lincoln craftsmen used lead filling, although it added 500 to 600 pounds to the car.

Because the trunk was too small, the spare tire was mounted on the trunk's exterior. Also to help speed the completion of the prototype, little trim was added to the exterior. The Continental looked sleek, especially when compared to GM cars, which were becoming beefier so they would look impressive on the road. The Continental didn't resemble a contemporary European-type design either, Gregorie recounted. The European custom bodies from Germany, for instance, tended to be "quite gaudy."

"I Could Sell a Thousand of Them"

The prototype Continental emerged from the Lincoln plant in March 1939 after a week of work. A rushed job, with an underpowered engine, inadequate brakes, and even leaks, it nonetheless looked stunning. It was painted gray, Edsel's favorite color, and had white sidewall tires and little chrome bumpers.

The car was shipped by truck to Hobe Sound, Florida, where Edsel was vacationing. Initially, Edsel intended to have three production cars built—one for himself, plus one each for his older sons, Henry II and Benson.

Fearful of reprisals from the Ford Service Department, about 1,000 Ford UAW members wore masks as they marched in Detroit's 1937 Labor Day Parade. *Walter Reuther Library, Wayne State University*

After driving the car for a couple of weeks, Edsel phoned Gregorie and said, "Gosh, I've driven this car around Palm Beach ... I could sell a thousand of them down here."

He wanted the Continental put into production as soon as possible, so an assembly line was set up in the Lincoln plant in an empty bay where craftsmen used to perform finishing work on the Lincoln K custom bodies. The car came out in 1940 as the Lincoln-Zephyr Continental Cabriolet, and by 1941 it was a distinct model.

Recovery and War

The U.S. economy improved in 1939 as indicated by motor vehicle registrations, which increased 4 percent to a total of 30.7 million vehicles. Despite the renewed federal government spending on jobs programs, the U.S. unemployment rate still exceeded 20 percent.

When Ford released its 1939 models, Edsel predicted that the automaker's sales would rebound to 750,000 units, a jump of nearly twofold over the 1938 totals. The actual results were

The 1939 De Luxe featured a "banjo"-style steering wheel with a die-cast hub and hard rubber rim. The horn button was chrome-plated and painted Zephyr Beige. The dashboard looks well planned, but it was designed in a single day after an oversight was discovered at the last moment. *The Henry Ford*

far lower and paled in comparison to GM and Chrysler. When 1939 ended, Ford sold 481,496 vehicles. For its first year, Mercury did well, selling 65,884 cars, while Lincoln sold 19,940 units, the vast majority of which were Zephyrs (only 133 were K Models).

For 1939, Chevrolet alone outsold Ford with 598,341 units. GM's total domestic sales were nearly 1.35 million units—about three times that of Ford.

The competition between Chevrolet and Ford was "the most dramatic show in the industry" with Chrysler's Plymouth brand making the contest more intense, noted *Fortune* magazine. In total U.S. car and truck registrations, Ford and Chevrolet were about neck and neck, with Ford holding a slim lead at 9.1 million units to some 9 million Chevys.

After the completion of the 24-stud V-8 engine project, at Edsel Ford's urging, attention turned to the creation of a new six-cylinder engine. Sheldrick started working on a conventional inline motor with an L-head and a distributor. When Henry heard of the project, he attempted to stop it, but then ordered Eugene Farkas to make a parallel design. Sheldrick's creation would eventually be put into production in 1941.

As Ford got ready to unveil its 1940 models, the Second Sino-Japanese War, which began with the Japanese invasion of China in 1937, brought America and the Empire of Japan closer to conflict. In Europe, England and France put their industries—including automotive factories—on a war-preparation footing to counter the military threats of Nazi Germany and the Soviet Union. Peace was shattered with the German and Soviet invasions of Poland in September 1939 as the two totalitarian nations touched off World War II.

Ford executive Jack Davis (right) presents actor Mickey Rooney with the keys to a new 1940 Lincoln-Zephyr Continental Cabriolet. Rooney portrayed Thomas Edison in *Young Tom Edison,* which was partially filmed in Michigan. Edison, who died in 1931, had been Henry Ford's friend and hero. *The Henry Ford*

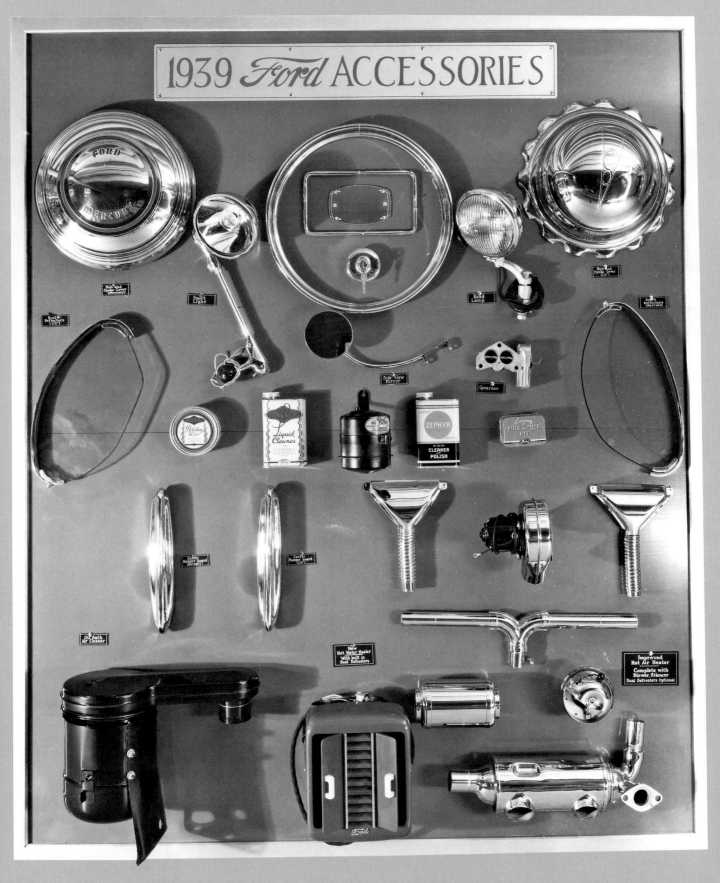

Some Ford accessories available for the 1939 model year included oil filters, special hubcaps, hot-water and hot-air heaters, side-view mirrors, spotlights, polish, cleaners, and more. *The Henry Ford*

Chapter Four

Ford for Forty

The possibility of war in Europe was on everybody's mind in the late 1930s. Leading off the 1938–1939 season at the Economic Club of Detroit, speaker Sir Herbert Ames—a member of the Canadian House of Commons and expert on European matters—talked about "What Does Fascism Mean to Europe and America?" Some of the other proposed titles for his speech were "Is Hitler Planning a War of Conquest?" or "Can Another Major European War Be Avoided—And If So, How?" or "Is Hitler Planning to Become the Twentieth Century Napoleon?"

By August 1939, Nazi Germany made aggressive statements about regaining the "Polish corridor"—territory lost after World War I when Poland was reconstituted following the Treaty of Versailles. Roosevelt sent urgent messages to Berlin, Warsaw, and Rome in an effort to avert war. Meanwhile Henry Ford thought the crisis was folly. "They don't dare have a war and they know it," he said some three days before German tanks rolled into Poland.

Sixteen days after Germany's Blitzkrieg into Poland, on September 17, 1939, the Soviet Union invaded the eastern third of the country and occupied Lithuania, Latvia, and Estonia. There followed a seven-month period on the Western Front known as the "Phony War." There was little fighting between the Allies (France and Great Britain) and Germany (Italy didn't join the war until June 10, 1940). During the winter of 1939–1940, Hitler told Britain and France to accept the conquest of Poland, but both countries refused.

Instead of traveling abroad, Americans tended to stay home or attended the New York and San Francisco world's fairs. As the world plunged back into war, Ford Motor Company slid into a power struggle between Edsel Ford and Harry Bennett while a renewed United Auto Workers pressured the company for acceptance.

The Fabulous '40 Fords
Ford had a successful 1939 summer sales program while nearly five million people flocked to its specially built exhibit halls at the two world's fairs, including 1.13 million people who went on the "Road of Tomorrow," an elevated highway that encircled Ford's New York hall. Riding the wave of good news, general sales manager Jack Davis proudly showed off the 1940 models to dealers and company sales managers in Dearborn during the last week of September 1939. The cars did not have any radical changes, but a number of defects had been remedied.

Improvements included a new fingertip gearshift on the steering column, sealed-beam headlights, better brakes, changes to the suspension system, and more. Seeing the cars demonstrated on the Dearborn test track, dealers initially ordered some 40,000 units. Davis set the coming year's sales goal at 900,000 vehicles, about double 1939's level.

The automaker also planned to build more than 250,000 Ford and Mercury cars before the beginning of 1940, a 44 percent increase from the year prior.

Ford's 1940 models included the Lincoln, the final year for the big K Model; an upgraded Lincoln-Zephyr that included the Continental Cabriolet and a V-12 engine that generated an extra 10 horsepower (120 horsepower at 3,500 rpm, specifically); the Mercury Eight; the Ford De Luxe V-8; and the Ford V-8. This also was the last year that the De Luxe and standard V-8s had distinctive front ends. Production of the V-8-60 ended in America after 1940, though the engine remained in production in Europe for several years after World War II. The Ford De Luxe came with the 85-horsepower engine as standard equipment, while the standard Ford had the "thrifty sixty" with the V-8-85 offered as an option.

Once again, the De Luxe grille was altered, having chrome-plated horizontal bars. The standard grille was a reworked 1939 De Luxe grille with vertical bars painted in body color except for the chrome-plated center strip. Ford still did not have a distinguishing grille motif, but the lack of a trademark grille was hardly a unique problem to Ford. Chevrolet only settled on a grille pattern by 1940. Cadillac didn't have a long lasting theme until its 1941 model.

Bracketing the Market
On October 2, 1939, the Ford V-8, Mercury Eight, and Zephyr lines were unveiled to newspaper and magazine writers who

Facing: It is October 6, 1940, at the Rotunda in Dearborn and the new 1940 models have been unveiled to the public. Simultaneous showings occurred around the country, including at the New York and San Francisco world's fairs. Visible in this picture are Ford De Luxes, Mercury Eights, and Lincoln-Zephyrs. Ford wanted to sell 900,000 units for the year, but several events, including the sudden demotion of general sales manager Jack Davis, blunted this rosy projection. *The Henry Ford* drove the cars on the Dearborn test track, toured the Village Industries (the event was recorded as a promotional film), and enjoyed a barbecue outside the Rotunda. The public saw the new cars four days after the press with introductions at the Golden Gate International Exposition and the New York World's Fair, where the models appeared on the "Road of Tomorrow."

Ford now had five cars bracketing the market. William J. Trepagnier, editor of AAA's *Motor News*, noted in its October 1939 issue that they "present many advances in styling, comfort and safety." One of these advances was sealed-beam headlights—one sealed unit comprising the lens, light bulb, and reflector. Thanks to a major cooperative effort between the automakers, lighting suppliers, and the American Association of

Motor Vehicle Administrators, sealed-beam headlights became the industry's standard in 1940. The new lights were brighter at night and retained their efficiency (older headlamps lost more than half of their efficiency after three years), giving drivers an extra degree of safety on the roads. Around the headlights, the standard V-8's rims were made of stainless steel and painted in the body color; the De Luxe's headlight rims were made of chrome-plated zinc die-cast steel.

The 1940 Mercury had various minor improvements, including a stabilizer bar and improved shock absorbers. The Convertible Sedan was added to the Mercury's lineup that included the Town Sedan, Sedan, Sedan Coupe, and Club Convertible. The 100,000th Mercury Eight came off the Rouge

For 1940, the Ford De Luxe grille was altered once again as seen on this Fordor Sedan sporting chrome-plated horizontal bars. Among its various other improvements, the car also has sealed-beam headlights for improved nighttime vision. Many consider the "Fabulous Forty Ford" to be the ultimate expression of the car line that started with the 1933 Ford. *The Henry Ford*

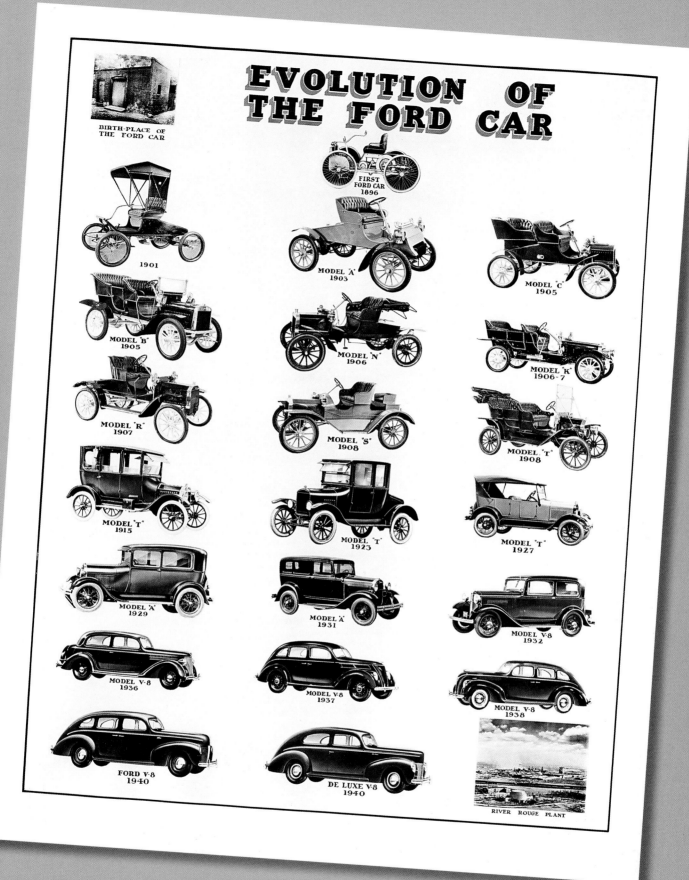

EVOLUTION OF THE FORD CAR

BIRTH-PLACE OF THE FORD CAR

FIRST FORD CAR 1896

1901

MODEL "A" 1903

MODEL "C" 1905

MODEL "B" 1905

MODEL "N" 1906

MODEL "K" 1906-7

MODEL "R" 1907

MODEL "S" 1908

MODEL "T" 1908

MODEL "T" 1915

MODEL "T" 1923

MODEL "T" 1927

MODEL "A" 1929

MODEL "A" 1931

MODEL V-8 1932

MODEL V-8 1936

MODEL V-8 1937

MODEL V-8 1938

FORD V-8 1940

DE LUXE V-8 1940

RIVER ROUGE PLANT

This chart shows the evolution of Ford's car designs from the 1896 horseless buggy called the Quadricycle to the 1903 Model A, various years of the Model T, the 1929 Model A, and the 1932 through 1940 V-8s. *Detroit Public Library, National Automotive History Collection*

Long before the 1940 Ford, Mercury Eight, or the Lincoln-Zephyr appeared in dealer showrooms, and before the first production car drove off the assembly line, every part of the cars underwent exhaustive tests on the company's new test track, which was created after overwhelming necessity finally intersected with Henry Ford's whims. General Motors had already dedicated testing facilities to improve their automobiles with technical advances. Ford's lack of a facility became a source of deep embarrassment for company executives and engineers.

In late 1936, truck designer Dale Roeder was driving Edsel and Henry Ford on Monroe Avenue in western Dearborn when Henry asked him where car testing was being done. Turning eastward, onto a connecting road to Oakwood Boulevard, Roeder replied that it had been done on public roads, which was an increasingly dangerous practice; the police also had complained to the company.

As Roeder turned onto Oakwood and approached the gate to Ford Airport, opposite the Dearborn Inn (one of America's first airport hotels and built by Henry Ford), Henry pointed to the airport and said, "Turn in here."

Roeder complied. They drove around the 425-acre airport (then a fair size for an airfield, though it pales in comparison to the modern-day Detroit Metropolitan Wayne County Airport, which is about 6,400 acres). Looking around,

Henry added, "We will have a test track in here."

Testing began immediately on the airport runways. During the Depression, few airplanes came into Ford Airport. When a pilot wanted to land or take off he would radio the field's office. An alarm would sound and the test drivers would scurry off the runways, noted John Côté Dahlinger, who worked as one of the drivers during the summers of his late teens.

The first dedicated automotive test track was laid at the airport by 1938. The growing facility was built under the direction of Ray Dahlinger, who oversaw the Ford Farms and the airport. Ford Airport remained in operation concurrent with automotive testing until 1947. (The son of Evangeline Dahlinger, John Dahlinger called Ray his dad, but in his 1978 autobiography, *The Secret Life of Henry Ford*, he claimed to be Henry Ford's illegitimate son.)

The test track included sections to simulate various road conditions, including wet roads, washboard roads, flooded roads, shifting sand, foot-deep mud, and even bricks and Belgian cobblestone. Tests included continuous 24-hour runs at low speeds, 90-mile-per-hour dashes around a 2 1/2-mile high-speed bowl, and runs over the "body twist" and "torture" tracks. The two-lane high-speed track was built around the runways and had banked curves to make turning relatively safe. Cars traversed the body twist and torture track at various speeds. There was even a 300-foot-long trough filled with 18 inches of water

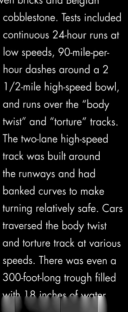

to simulate flooded roads, plus a 200-foot-long "mud bath" where cars passed through a slough up to 10 inches deep.

The effect of several trips over these surfaces simulated thousands of miles of everyday driving so Ford could build better products.

Another part of the testing facility was a wind tunnel in the old air frame building on the airport property. With massive air fans capable of simulating wind velocities as high as 80 miles an hour, it could also produce great heat, temperatures as low as 20 degrees below zero Fahrenheit, and imitation rainstorms and other conditions. Adjacent to the wind tunnel was a special cold room, where temperatures could plunge to 40 below zero to help research the performance of batteries, starters, and carburetors under arctic-like conditions.

Above: A 1941 Mercury Eight enters a simulated arctic freeze on August 22, 1940, at Ford's new wind tunnel facility in the old air frame building at Ford Airport in Dearborn. *The Henry Ford*

Left: A 1940 Ford Standard Sedan takes on a 300-foot-long trough simulating flooded roads. Ford's first testing facility also had a 200-foot-long "mud bath," a high-speed bowl track, and courses to simulate various road conditions. *The Henry Ford*

Despite the gathering efforts of the UAW-CIO to organize Ford workers, production continued on cars inside the "B" Building, the Rouge's assembly plant. Two stations away from where the body is dropped onto the chassis, a worker appears to be making adjustments to the sealed-beam headlight. *Walter P. Reuther Library, Wayne State University*

This advertisement ran in Sunday newspapers on May 5 and 12, 1940, touting how Ford cars were ahead of the competition. *The Henry Ford*

assembly line on January 18, 1940. In less than 16 months since its introduction, the car was one of the top 10 cars sold in America.

Meeting consumer demands, Ford cars also were equipped with a fingertip shift lever mounted on the steering column; however, Ford lagged its major competitors. GM and Chrysler had first offered optional column shifters in 1938 and 1939, respectively. The V-8s' transverse leaf springs were lengthened to soften the ride, while an anti-roll/stabilizer bar was introduced for better steering. Notably, transverse leaf springs were phased out of most Ford trucks for 1940, showing that Henry was no longer fully involved with approving all vehicle designs.

"Ford's designers—with the Lincoln Continental, the Zephyr, the Mercury, and the '40 Ford—created a fine balance between being streamlined and having beautiful aesthetics. They

Right: The stylized hubcaps of the 1940 Standard featured "V-8" painted in blue. The hubcaps on the De Luxe model were stamped "FORD De Luxe" with the letters painted red or maroon. Outer trim rings were standard equipment, but inner rings were optional. *The Henry Ford*

Below: A 1940 De Luxe rolling chassis is pictured on July 12, 1939. When the body is mounted, the finished car's overall length will be 15 inches longer than the 1933 model, but it will retain a 112-inch wheelbase and have similar body lines. Most Ford frames were 0.10 inches thick, the exception being the frames of most convertibles and Station Wagons, which were 0.11 inches because they had less rigid bodies. Visible in this view are the X-member, torque-tube driveshaft, 24-stud V-8-85 engine, carburetor, radiator, and other components. *The Henry Ford*

are an incredible group of cars," noted automotive designer Larry Erickson.

Ultimate Expression

Although 15 inches longer overall, the 1940 Ford was in many ways the ultimate expression of its 1933 predecessor. The 1933 through 1940 Ford models had the same 112-inch wheelbase and a similar chassis. Buyers had little trouble recognizing the basic lines of the 1940 car. The body styles for the 60-horsepower series were the Coupe, Business Coupe, and Tudor and Fordor Sedans. They ranged in price from $620 to $700. The 85-horsepower standard series added the Station Wagon; prices were from $640 to $850. The De Luxe V-8 added the

The four-seat Club Coupe had disappeared from Ford's lineup for 1940, but the Standard and De Luxe models offered two rear jump seats (popularly called "opera seats") with a padded rear rail as a backrest in place of a rear shelf. The front seats of "Opera Coupes" also folded away to allow easier access to the back. This style was popular with businessmen transporting sales samples and with families with children. *The Henry Ford*

A woman applies makeup while looking at the optional sun visor vanity mirror in a 1940 Ford Coupe. Vanity mirrors and other equipment were standard on special two-tone De Luxe models. *The Henry Ford*

Convertible Club Coupe; models were priced from $700 to $920. The Mercury's starting price was $920 for the Two Door Sedan up to $1,180 for the Convertible Sedan. The Lincoln-Zephyr started at $1,360 for the Three Passenger Coupe up to $2,840 for the Continental Cabriolet.

The five-window Ford Business Coupe gave buyers the option of a package tray in back or two folding jump seats with a padded rear rail as a back rest (this version was nicknamed the Opera Coupe and was popular with traveling salesmen and owners who transported children or small adults in the back). The coupe's front seats featured a split back and folded to provide access to the rear. The Convertible Club Coupe had a vacuum-powered top similar to what Plymouth had debuted in 1939 and what Chevrolet offered for 1940.

Buyers could order the De Luxe in seven colors: Acadia Green, Black, Cloud Mist Gray, Folkstone Gray, Lyon Blue, Yosemite Green, and Mandarin Maroon. The special spring color was Garnet (a lighter shade of maroon). Buyers also could get two-tone cars such as a Folkstone Gray body and wheels with Black or Mandarin Maroon fenders and grille sides; a Mandarin Maroon body and wheels with Folkstone Gray fenders and grille sides; or a Cloud Mist Gray body and wheels with Acadia Green fenders and grille sides. The two-tone cars' standard equipment included license plate frames, fender skirts, locking gas tank cap, visor vanity mirror, oil-bath air cleaner and filter, wheel trim rings, seat covers or leather seats, radio, heater, and bumper end and center guards. The standard V-8 came in three colors: Black, Cloud Mist Gray, and Lyon Blue. Except for the two-tone cars, the wheels on all Fords were painted black, but for an extra charge, they could be had in a matching body color.

Ford offered either a hot-air or a hot-water heater for its passenger cars. Optional radios came either from Philco or Zenith. Again following GM's and Chrysler's lead, the Fords

One of the neatest looking convertibles in the pre–World War II era was the 1940 Ford De Luxe Coupe. Equipped with the new fingertip gearshift, ventilation windows, and sealed-beam headlights, it was priced at $800. *The Henry Ford*

THE FORD V·8 *Station Wagons*

The DeLuxe Ford V-8 Station Wagon

This ad for the 1940 De Luxe Station Wagon perhaps took inspiration from the model's genesis in Michigan's rugged Upper Peninsula. *Motorbooks collection*

incorporated front-door vent windows. At the back, the Forty Fords received chevron-styled taillights instead of the teardrop style that had been on the 1937–1939 models.

New disc wheels and improved drums were added for the hydraulic brakes. The hubcaps on the standard car were stamped with a stylized "V8"with blue lettering. The De Luxe cars were stamped "FORD De Luxe" and had either red or maroon lettering. New hydraulic shock absorbers were installed along with more flexible front and rear transverse leaf springs, which had metal coverings to help keep them lubricated. Because the softer springs increased the car's roll during cornering maneuvers, Ford installed an antiroll bar (which was also placed on the Mercury and Zephyr) as a way to tie down the front axle at the outer ends.

Despite the improvements to its suspension, many buyers thought Ford's ride quality was inferior to GM and Chrysler cars that had perfected so-called "flat rides" and had good roll resistance.

Inside, the Ford V-8s received the two-spoke steering wheel, similar to the 1939 Mercury, and a new instrument panel with a rounded dash. Mounted on the panel were the starter, headlight beam indicator, a built-in grille to ease the installation of an optional radio, and a locking glove compartment.

The standard Ford had a single sheet of glass covering the gauges, bleached walnut for the door and window moldings, chrome-plated and sand-colored plastic interior hardware, a new battery-condition indicator, twin electric air horns, and dual windshield wipers. In addition to the Standard's equipment, the De Luxe had a plastic fascia for the gauges, a clock, windows and door frames finished in dark mahogany, and maroon-colored handles.

The De Luxe's upholstery was available as either striped mohair or fine-quality broadcloth. The Convertible Club Coupe had saddle brown leather seats. Other leather seating options included light tan (maple), reddish brown (mahogany), and Red Mercury leather. The driver's seat could be raised and also

These are Ford Station Wagon body parts for the Models 74 and 78-790 for 1937. By 1940, workers at the Iron Mountain plant used about 445 board feet of lumber, cutting, sanding, and fashioning the wood into 150 pieces for each body. The plywood panels were made from gumwood; the frames used birch and maple; roof slats were fashioned from basswood. Workers joined the wood to 750 other metal body components that had been shipped via freight train from the Rouge. *The Henry Ford*

slid forward a total of 4 1/2 inches. Smokers were given two ashtrays—one for the driver and one for the front passenger.

Utility and Sharp Looks

Created to meet utilitarian purposes, the Ford Station Wagon evolved in 1937 when safety-glass windows replaced the snap-on window curtains used in earlier models. Initially, engineers, surveyors, telephone maintenance and repair crews, scientific expeditions, and owners of large estates were the primary markets for the cars, but buyer interest grew markedly between 1938 and 1939. For 1940, Ford and its competitors gave their wagons more detailed attention, thus combining utility with sharp looks.

The Station Wagon became the 1940 Standard and De Luxe V-8's top-of-the-line model. Five hundred miles north of Detroit, in Michigan's rugged Upper Peninsula, the 300 woodworkers at Ford's Iron Mountain plant made 75 to 80 bodies a day. Using hardwood timbers harvested from nearby Ford-owned lands, workers cut, sanded, and fashioned about 445 board feet of lumber into the 150 pieces needed for each body. The plywood panels

Originally created to meet utilitarian purposes, by 1940 Ford's Station Wagons became the top-of-the-line model for the Standard and De Luxe V-8 lines. Ford's Iron Mountain plant made 75 to 80 bodies a day using hardwoods from the forests of Michigan's Upper Peninsula. The varnished body and hardware was hand-rubbed until it assumed a "piano finish." This De Luxe Station Wagon appears to be at the passenger terminal of Ford Airport in Dearborn. Fleet buyers like the U.S. government could order the wagon with the 95-horsepower Mercury V-8. *The Henry Ford*

A billboard depicting a man atop a telephone pole lets everyone know that he's using a Ford truck. Among the 40 improvements to Ford's commercial vehicles were sealed-beam headlights, larger batteries and generators, and the elimination of transverse leaf springs except on the half-ton chassis, which received a heavier steel frame. *The Henry Ford*

A 1940 Ford heavy-duty tractor owned by the Snoqualmie Falls Lumber Company hauls timber out of the Washington State forest where teams of horses were once needed for logging operations. Ford's commercial truck owners had the choice of upgrading their V-8-85s to the new Mercury 95-horsepower engine with a two-speed axle for more power. *The Henry Ford*

were made from gum wood; the frames used birch and maple; roof slats were fashioned from basswood. Workers joined the wood to 750 other metal body components—including steel stampings for the floor pan, cowls, housings for the wheels, and windshield frames—that had been shipped via freight train from the Rouge.

Dusty from their journey, the unpainted steel parts were washed in acid baths to remove grime and rust, then hot-water sprays removed the acid. Afterward, workers set the steel parts on a conveyor that took them under the intense heat of 800 infrared, 250-watt drying lamps.

Once dry, parts were cleaned with alcohol to remove oxidation and then rubbed dry again. The welding department took the floor sections as painters worked on other parts. After all the metal parts received their primary coats of paint, sanding, and a second coat of enamel, the assembly operations began.

The 1940 Ford pickup truck took on the look of the Ford Standard passenger cars. Trucks painted with two tones could be ordered with the 60-, 85-, or 95-horsepower V-8s. This photo was taken September 14, 1939, at Greenfield Village's Smith Creek train station. Originally located on the tracks leading to Port Huron, Michigan, it was one of the stops where a young Thomas Edison sold newspapers. *The Henry Ford*

Right: A 134-inch-wheelbase 1940 Ford stake truck is pictured alongside the Rouge's piers where Great Lakes ore boats delivered their cargo. Visible in the background are one of the tugs and barges of the Ford Fleet, which numbered about 30 vessels before most were requisitioned by the federal government for the war effort. *The Henry Ford*

Below: The 1940 122-inch-wheelbase "one-tonner" was offered in seven body and chassis types, such as this Panel Delivery Truck. Ford's truck front ends were restyled with massive grilles but graceful contours. Panel truck bodies also were available on the 112-inch chassis, as a "three-quarter tonner" on the 122-inch chassis, and on the 134-inch chassis. All units were equipped with hydraulic brakes, sealed-beam headlights, easier access to check water and oil levels, new generators with voltage regulators, bigger batteries, and a cargo area that could be ordered with wooden slats or Masonite paneling. *The Henry Ford*

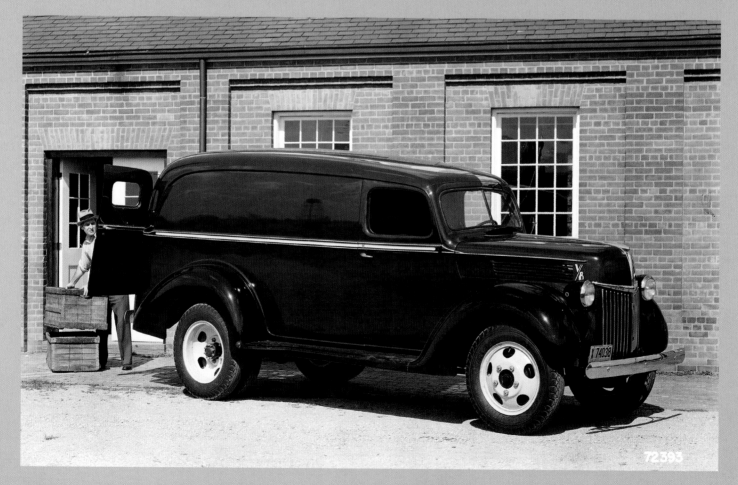

The bodies were varnished and polished twice with trips into the 125-degree Fahrenheit drying oven tunnels equipped with 1,600 infrared lamps.

"The hardware body is again hand-rubbed until it assumes a 'piano finish,'" noted *Ford News* in its March 1940 issue. "The unit is washed thoroughly, inside and out, with naphtha gas. Every joint and fitting receives a final inspection under brilliant light."

Using a framing fixture known as a body buck, workers placed the floor piece in first. Then a half-dozen men along the assembly line installed the cowl, windshield assemblies, pillars, and other wood parts. The body was temporarily bolted to skids to prevent distortion as side panels and doors were installed. The body rapidly took shape with the addition of tailgates, safety-glass windows, hardware, and electrical fixtures.

At the trim line, workers added the remaining interior and exterior components, including the seats. Artificial leather, made at Highland Park, was used in all standard Station Wagons while genuine leather was used for De Luxe models. Inspectors diverted one out of every ten bodies for a more thorough check because variations of fractions of an inch would cause doors to be misaligned and other problems.

All Station Wagon bodies were submitted to five minutes under myriad water sprays at 60 pounds of pressure and checked for leaks. The completed bodies were then loaded into boxcars and shipped to Ford assembly plants.

The notorious drawback of the woody wagons was their high maintenance; the bodies needed to be re-varnished every year or the wood deteriorated. The fabric roof also required frequent re-coatings and replacement. After World War II, the automakers transitioned to all-steel station wagons.

Trucks with Power

Ford's 1940 commercial vehicles were similar to the previous year's models. It offered 42 body and chassis types, 6 wheelbases, and 3 V-8 engines. Among the 40 improvements were items such as sealed-beam headlights, larger batteries and generators, and the elimination of transverse leaf springs, except for the half-ton chassis (which received a heavier steel frame). The new longitudinal front leaf springs, similar to those previously installed on the cab-over-engine trucks, allowed mechanics easier access to the engine from underneath and made it simpler to install special equipment and service the clutch, transmission, universal joints, and rear axle.

Most Ford trucks received the 1939 Ford De Luxe's front-end styling. The surface area of the radiators was enlarged, but the capacity was reduced from 24 to 22 quarts. Other changes included lowering the floor of the 112-inch-wheelbase stake truck to increase the load space, while the bus chassis was increased to a 194-inch wheelbase.

How could we ever have Christmas without Ford V·8 Trucks?

All over town, they're hauling things — big trucks, little trucks, middle-size trucks — delivering packages from the stores . . . bringing in cordwood and Christmas trees, chickens and turkeys from the country . . . carrying big shipments of merchandise from city to city. It's hard to find a single hauling or delivery job that Ford V-8 Trucks don't handle today.

The 42 different body and chassis types comprising the 1940 line of trucks and commercial cars, in TIME, December 11, 1939

combination with a choice of engines — 95, 85 and 60 hp — make it possible to select the exact unit that will do more work for you — in less time, at lower cost.

There are lots of improvements in the new Ford Truck, and a host of time-tested Ford features that mean one thing—*quality!* See these units at your Ford dealer's and compare them with any other truck at any price. Arrange for an actual "on-the-job" test and find out for yourself the difference Ford quality

and Ford economy make before you spend another truck dollar.

Ford Motor Company, builders of Ford V-8 and Mercury Cars, Ford Trucks, Commercial Cars, Station Wagons and Transit Buses

FORD V·8 TRUCKS AND COMMERCIAL CARS

31

Ford used the holidays as an entrée to consumers' good senses — and presumably their heart strings — when touting their broad lineup of 1940 trucks. *Motorbooks collection*

Troubling Headwinds

The automaker's sales momentum, however, was beset with many troubling headwinds. There were clashes with labor and the federal government, and the competition wasn't standing still. Ford Motor Company's 1940 sales rose to 644,162 units, including 542,755 of the tough Ford V-8 cars and trucks and 80,418 Mercurys. The rest were mostly Lincoln-Zephyrs, which were declining in overall sales (the Zephyr marque wouldn't come back after the war). Although sales were up from 1939, it was a far cry from Ford's goal of 900,000 units.

Chevrolet and Plymouth offered buyers all-new vehicles with more up-to-date mechanics that were priced very close to the Fords. The Plymouths had some of Chrysler's best prewar engineering feats such as "Luxury Ride" (which redistributed the car's weight to provide more of a balance between the front and the back), improved steering and transmission, a heavier frame, and standard coil springs for the front independent suspension. In addition, it had grown to a 117-inch wheelbase. Sales were nearly a half-million units.

The 1940 Chevrolet was an advanced car with a large and more spacious body and a 113-inch wheelbase, presenting an impressive-looking front end. It sold 894,178 units for the year alone.

The Road of Tomorrow

Within four days of the press previews for the 1940 Ford, on October 6, 1939, the automaker introduced its vehicles to the public at Hotel Astor, where an estimated 22,000 people saw the cars on the first day. (The event was concurrent with the 1939 New York Auto Show.) What's more, the new Fords, Mercurys, and Lincoln-Zephyrs simultaneously appeared to visitors at the New York World's Fair and the San Francisco Golden

Wartime has yet to come to America during the early summer of 1940 as Baroness Alice Stael von Holstein of Stockholm visits the Ford Exposition at the New York World's Fair and sits behind the wheel of the 1940 Lincoln-Zephyr Continental Cabriolet on display in the Garden Court. Known as Sweden's leading woman driver, the baroness was a member of the Royal Auto Club of Sweden and had driven over most of the European continent. The war interrupted her plans to take her Ford on a tour of Tibet and South Africa. *The Henry Ford*

Soaring up a spiral ramp that ascends 33 feet in a short span, the "Road of Tomorrow" was a winding double-lane path of cork and rubber in Ford's exhibition building at the 1939–1940 World's Fair. The building had a red-white-and-blue color scheme. Along with the roadway, the exhibit showcased manufacturing activities, featured stylized displays created by industrial designer Walter Dorwin Teague, and

N.Y 221

Glenn H. Merithew was one of 48 boys competing in the two-day finals for the Ford Good Drivers League at the New York World's Fair. The league was created to promote better driving, and the winner received a $5,000 college scholarship. Here Merithew zigzags a Ford De Luxe Tudor Sedan through rows of posts set up at odd angles. The league was opened up for girls in 1941. *The Henry Ford*

Gate International Exposition, where tens of thousands more saw them.

The world's fairs on the East and West Coasts were a brief respite for Americans after World War II broke out in Europe. In fact, Henry Ford had called them "an agency for peace and an inspiration for youth." New York fairgoers rode the cars on Ford's "The Road of Tomorrow"—part of its 7-acre exhibition center that came with a stylistic, 25-foot stainless-steel statue of the Roman god Mercury. Visitors saw scenes that depicted vast changes to rural and urban life brought about by mass production. Many of Ford's displays were designed by industrial artist Walter Dorwin Teague, including the "Ford Cycle of Production," which depicted how raw materials were refined and eventually fashioned into finished cars.

With the theme of "The World of Tomorrow" that promoted futuristic visions complete with the help of two central structures—the 18-story Perisphere and the 700-foot triangular obelisk called the Trylon—the New York fair ran

Singing cowboy Roy Rogers visited the Ford exhibit at the New York World's Fair on September 18, 1940. He's pictured here on the hood of a Mercury Sedan rather than on his iconic horse, Trigger. *The Henry Ford*

A "Typical American Family" with a typical American car. During the New York World's Fair, Ford held a special promotion that brought more than 40 families on an all-expenses-paid trip to the Big Apple in new Fords, such as this 1940 De Luxe Fordor Sedan. The families were selected in contests sponsored by large newspapers in several regions. While at the fair, the contestants stayed in specially built homes adjacent to the fair's "Town of Tomorrow" on Long Island. Each family group was limited to two adults and two children because the model homes were made to accommodate only four people. *The Henry Ford*

from April through October 1939 and then reopened for the April to October 1940 season.

Ford had the largest single commercial exhibit at the San Francisco fair, which was held on the manmade Treasure Island in San Francisco Bay. Celebrating the opening of the Golden Gate and the San Francisco–Oakland Bay bridges, the West Coast fair ran from February 18 until October 29, 1939, and reopened again for the May 25, 1940, to September 29, 1940, season.

Ford showcased vehicles such as the 100,000th Lincoln-Zephyr (a Continental Cabriolet model) at New York and sponsored the Good Drivers League program and a forum to search for young designers.

Additionally, both the 27 millionth Ford (a green 1939 De Luxe Tudor Sedan) and the 28 millionth Ford (a 1940 Fordor De Luxe) were shown in New York. The '39 Ford, which

symbolized that Ford had created one-third of all motor cars ever built, rolled off the final assembly line of the Richmond, California, plant in February 1939. It started at the San Francisco fair and was driven to New York, where it was met on June 16, 1939, by a group of dignitaries that included Henry, Clara, and Edsel Ford, and Mayor Fiorello H. LaGuardia. The car eventually circled back to San Francisco, completing an 8,854-mile circuit of the United States.

The 28 millionth Ford was completed April 8, 1940, at the automaker's Edgewater, New Jersey, plant. The '40 De Luxe Fordor Sedan first visited the New York fair before heading westward, stopping at various cities and state capitals, collecting license plates and autographs. The car was also driven to Mexico before appearing at the San Francisco fair and finally ended its journey in Vancouver, Canada. "This 28 millionth

Right: Even as tensions mounted between labor activists and Ford, headlines of the papers being sold at the Rouge's Gate 4 pedestrian bridge in 1940 show that many people probably had the war in Europe on their minds. *Dearborn Historical Museum*

Below: Ford drivers Jimmy Rooney and Jack Doyle stop at Cross Motor Sales in Bowling Green, Ohio, with the 27 millionth Ford. Rooney and Doyle were driving the green 1939 De Luxe Tudor Sedan from the San Francisco Golden Gate International Exposition to the New York World's Fair. The car was built at Ford's Richmond, California, plant in February 1939 and symbolized that the automaker had created one-third of all motor cars ever built. The car eventually circled back to San Francisco, completing a 8,854-mile circuit of America. *The Henry Ford*

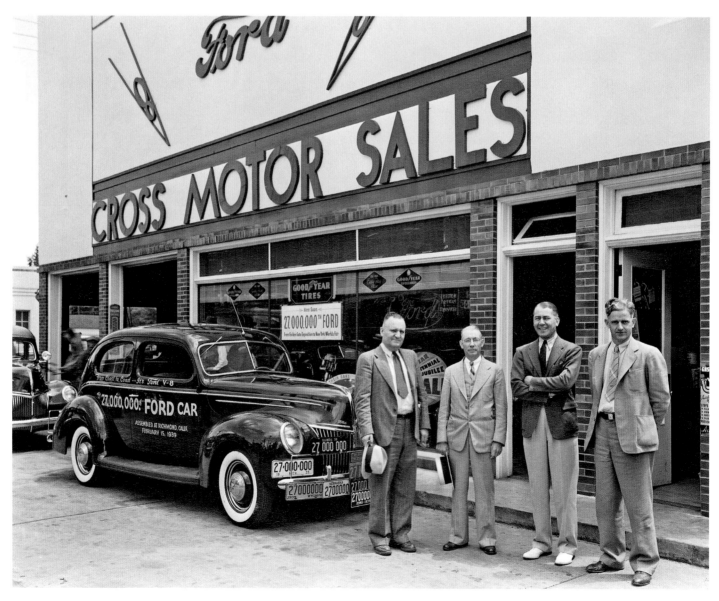

car is produced in a world war, but its first journey will be across two unfortified boundaries. . . . Some future car will see all fortified boundaries abolished, or preserved as relics of a barbarous past," said William Cameron, Ford spokesman as he talked on the *Ford Sunday Evening Hour* radio program on April 7, 1940, the night before the car was completed.

Officially headed by Edsel Ford, the Good Drivers League was created to promote better driving habits among high school boys (the program was expanded in 1941 to include teenage girls; after the war, the American Automobile Association, AAA, sponsored the program). More than 60,000 boys participated and finals were held in April 1940 at the New York fair. Contestants drove Ford cars, and winners were awarded $100 to $5,000 scholarships to 48 universities. The program no doubt helped sell cars, too, since entry forms had to be filled out at Ford, Lincoln, and Mercury dealers.

Another Ford promotional program was a nationwide contest featuring "Typical American Families" who traveled to the New York fair in new Ford cars.

Winds of War

Ford's wishes for peace were not to be. On April 9, 1940, the German army crashed into Denmark and Norway. Before the end of June, the French surrendered, leaving England alone against the Axis. Next came the Battle of Britain with the German air force bombing English industrial centers, including the Ford plant at Dagenham, during the summer and autumn months. Ford's factories, like those of many multinational companies, including GM, were located on both sides of the conflict.

Officially neutral when the war started, America was divided between a camp that included President Roosevelt and others who pushed for a military buildup and those such as Henry Ford, aviator Charles Lindbergh, and Father Charles Coughlin, who argued for a more isolationist approach. Henry had taken a similar view during World War I. With a new war

in Europe, Henry was willing to accept preparedness contracts for the defense of the United States, but he stuck with his pacifist principals.

On May 28, 1940, General Motors President William S. Knudsen left GM to become commissioner for industrial production. His new role was to help coordinate the nation's war preparedness operations. Detroit would be crucial to America's vast "Arsenal of Democracy." Among the projects that Edsel Ford and Charles Sorensen considered was a contract to produce Rolls-Royce motors on behalf of the U.S. government. Both were enthusiastic about the project, and Ford engineers hurriedly made preparations.

Suddenly, Henry Ford threw a proverbial monkey wrench into the works after Lord Beaverbrook, Great Britain's minister of aircraft production, announced that Ford was producing the engines for England. Meeting with Knudsen in June 1940, Henry said, "I won't make any of those Rolls-Royce engines for England."

"But, Mr. Ford, we have your word that you would make them," Knudsen said, taken aback. "I told the president of your decision, and he was very happy about it."

Henry wouldn't budge, especially when Roosevelt's name was mentioned. "We won't build the engines at all. Withdraw the whole order. Take it to someone else."

Knudsen left the meeting "purple with rage," Sorensen later recounted. (Packard readily accepted the Rolls-Royce project.)

According to Allan Nevins and Frank Hill in their 1963 book, *Ford: Decline and Rebirth 1933–1962*, after news of Ford's abandonment of the contract was made public, the company received a deluge of angry letters. Many letter writers vowed never to purchase another Ford car.

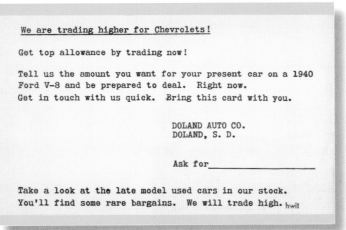

Above: Ford dealerships mailed postcards such as this to owners of used Chevrolets, urging them to trade in on a new '40 Ford or even a used Ford. *Motorbooks collection*

Ford, however, accepted other defense contracts, including making Pratt & Whitney aircraft engines and eventually producing 8,685 B-24 Liberator bombers (this contract led to the creation of the Willow Run bomber plant and airport on Ford farmland near Ypsilanti, Michigan). The company also submitted a proposal to build a light all-terrain vehicle (the jeep). Through all this, the UAW-CIO complained about Ford's participation in defense work because the company wasn't complying with federal government labor laws; Knudsen overrode labor's objections.

Only Ford, Willys-Overland, and a tiny car company called American Bantam placed bids on the army's contract for a four-wheel-drive, 75-inch-wheelbase vehicle that could carry 600 pounds yet weigh only about 1,200 pounds. Out of the three designs, American Bantam's was considered the best, but Willys' 60-horsepower "Go Devil" engine was a better powerplant. The government gave half of the production to Willys and half to Ford. American Bantam was stuck with building trailers that could be towed behind the vehicle they had designed. According to Laurence Sheldrick the name "jeep"—possibly a derivative of the initials "GP" for "general purpose"—originated at Ford, but that story has been disputed.

Next Generations

In autumn 1940, the next generation of Fords was introduced. The biggest car ever made by the brand, it weighed 3,419 pounds and had a 114-inch wheelbase. For the first time in decades, the Ford could be equipped with a six-cylinder engine. A V-8 was still offered, but the 60-horsepower engine was gone from the lineup. With large fenders and a big vertical grille, the 1941 Ford looked more impressive on the road. The Fordor Sedan, for example, was 7 inches wider than the previous model. The era of lightweight, peppy Fords that started with the 1932 models had ended.

After the Japanese attack on Pearl Harbor on December 7, 1941, America fully mobilized for war. Civilian car production ended when a Ford car came off the line on February 10, 1942, according to Russ Banham, writing in *The Ford Century*, Ford Motor Company's official centennial history. No new cars would be made until 1945, and many of the postwar cars were dolled up 1942 models. Ford would not have a new car design until mid-1948 when the slab-sided 1949 models were introduced.

Edsel Ford's ailments were finally diagnosed as stomach cancer, and surgeons removed half of his stomach in January 1942, but by then the malignancy had spread to his liver. As World War II raged, Edsel became sicker as he faced constant conflicts with Bennett. His health finally broke, and he died at age 49 on May 26, 1943.

The day before Edsel's funeral, the frail, nearly 80-year-old Henry Ford resumed the title and day-to-day responsibilities of company president much to the surprise of Sorensen and other executives. The management team began to break up with a

series of forced resignations, retirements, and firings. Ernest Liebold, Bob Gregorie, and Laurence Sheldrick were gone before March 1944; a month later, Sorensen resigned. He later took over Willys-Overland.

With control of Ford Motor Company teetering on collapse, the Roosevelt administration released Henry Ford II from his duties at the Naval Great Lakes Training Center in August 1943. (Before the attack on Pearl Harbor, Henry II and Benson had enlisted in the military.) At Ford, the 23-year-old Henry II found allies, including Jack Davis in California and Mead Bricker, who succeeded Sorensen in production. His mother, Eleanor Ford, and grandmother, Clara Ford, pressured old Henry to relinquish power to his grandson. About a month after the war's end, Henry II wrested control of the automaker away from Bennett and fired the "little man."

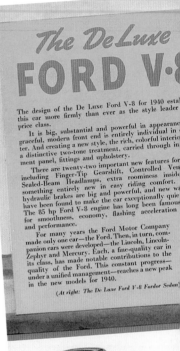

100

LUXE COUPE

DE LUXE CONVERTIBLE CLUB COUPE

DE LUXE BUSINESS COUPE

FORDOR SEDAN

COUPE

BUSINESS COUPE

The FORD V·8

The lower-priced Ford V-8, with a character of its own, is definitely modern in every detail of design. This is evident in the deep hood, the low grille, the long, smooth lines and the accent upon size and roominess.

Like the De Luxe Ford, it has advanced in value all along the line, with a great number of important new features.

It has the same extra inches of leg room, Finger-Tip Gearshift, Controlled Ventilation, Sealed-Beam Headlamps, and the same quiet, easy-shifting transmission. The improved shock absorbers, and the more flexible springs and new torsion bar ride-stabilizer on all 85 hp models, give it an outstandingly level ride. Its big hydraulic brakes give straight, quick stops.

Two V-8 engine sizes are available. With the 85 hp engine, for peak performance, the Ford is priced low—and still lower with the smaller 60 hp engine which emphasizes operating economy.

Whether you choose the Ford V-8 or the De Luxe Ford V-8, you know that the matchless experience and manufacturing facilities of the Ford Motor Company assure you of the best possible value for the money you invest.

(At left: The Ford V-8 Tudor Sedan)

Ford used this beautifully produced brochure to help roll out the new 1940 models. *Motorbooks collection*

Chapter Five

Balances of Power

„LA VOITURE SANS SOUCIS„

Although Germans Gottlieb Daimler and Karl Benz had demonstrated their gasoline-powered road conveyances in 1887, for many reasons—including European laws that discouraged automotive use—Americans were much quicker to embrace the car. Even with the financial deprivations of the Great Depression, by the mid-1930s there was an average of one motorized vehicle for every five persons in the United States. Outside of North America, the average was only one car to every 187 people. Europe didn't catch up until well after World War II.

The 1930s witnessed both the creation and splintering of Ford's plan to use its Dagenham, England, plant as the "Rouge of Europe." Ford proudly marketed its cars under the Ford, Lincoln, and later Mercury names. It had a distinctively American identity in Europe, whereas its major American rival, General Motors, bought European car companies such as Opel in Germany and Vauxhall in England.

Henry Ford strongly believed that the Model A and then V-8 would be the keys to winning in Europe, but the strategy failed. Under Great Britain's horsepower tax, for example, the Model A's engine was considered too large, which led to the creation of the four-cylinder Ford Model Y, the first car designed by Bob Gregorie. Yet, on the cobblestone roads of Belgium, the "Y" received the disparaging nickname "springing goat" and did not sell well. Buyers in Belgium, the Netherlands, and Sweden preferred larger cars, such as the Ford V-8.

Sir Percival Perry's Imperial Dreams

Ford became an international company in 1904, the year after its founding, when Henry Ford authorized Canadian entrepreneur Gordon McGregor to create Ford of Canada in Walkerville, Ontario, just across the river from Detroit. The arrangement allowed Ford to avoid the Dominion of Canada's 35 percent import duty, but more importantly, McGregor obtained the right to sell Fords throughout the British Empire.

In England, Ford's first tiny branch assembly plant opened in an old tramcar factory at Trafford Park, south of Manchester, in October 1911, while a British dealer named Sir Percival Lea Dewhurst Perry wanted the United Kingdom to be Ford's major European manufacturing center. Following World War I, Perry suggested that Ford build a factory in England—to be the European version of the Rouge. When his plans were frustrated, Perry resigned.

In 1922, Ford purchased more than 600 acres of marshy land on the north bank of the Thames River about 12 miles east of London at Dagenham, but nothing happened at the site until six years later when Henry rehired Perry to become the chairman of a new Ford Motor Company, Ltd. (a.k.a., Ford of England). Under his "1928 Plan," Perry would get his Rouge of Europe and oversee the automaker's sales and branch assembly plants in Belgium, Denmark, Finland, France, Germany, Holland, Spain, and Sweden. Eventually, Perry's purview extended to sales territories in the Middle East, North Africa, Greece, Italy, and Portugal.

As Perry's imperial dreams came close to fulfillment, the Depression, nationalistic trade policies, and executive whimsies in Dearborn ripped the 1928 Plan to shreds. Perry's authority over the European subsidiaries eroded as the German and French companies reported to Edsel Ford and Charles Sorensen, wanting to deal directly with the Americans rather than their English lieutenant.

Construction began in May 1929 on the massive Dagenham industrial center, which, like the Rouge, had its own steel mills, one of the largest blast furnaces in Britain that made 500 tons of pig iron a day, plus an 1,800-foot-long jetty to handle oceangoing freighters. About 200,000 piles had to be sunk 80 feet into the marshy ground to support the engine and car factories.

Initially, Dagenham was supposed to produce 250,000 cars annually with half of its vehicles slated for export to continental Europe. However, as protectionist tariffs rose in Europe, Ford trimmed the plant's capacity to 120,000 units (prewar production peaked in 1937 at 77,830 units) including a number of knockdown car kits. Like the Rouge, raw materials were brought in at one end of the plant, and finished Ford cars, trucks, and tractors came out the other to be loaded onto ships that resembled floating garages.

To control its international subsidiaries, Ford set up a complex system that historians Mira Wilkins and Frank Ernest Hill called a "financial whirligig." Ford Motor Company owned

Facing: A colorful ad showing either a Matford 3.6 Type F 81 A or a 2.2 Type F 82 A (the models look very similar) characterizes the vehicle as *La Voiture sans Soucis,* or "The Car without Worry." Under Maurice Dollfus, the French-produced V-8s went upmarket, and advertising stressed the cars' luxury qualities. *Michael W. MacSems collection*

59 percent of Ford England, which owned 60 percent of Ford Denmark, which owned 60 percent of Ford Sweden, which owned 60 percent of Ford Finland. The remaining shares were sold to individuals in those nations. The confusing arrangement permitted foreign countries to tax the company's overseas profits at almost every level.

A Model AA truck was the first vehicle to roll off Dagenham's assembly line on October 1, 1931. The first passenger car was the Model AF—basically a Model A equipped with a 14.9–British horsepower engine (this figure represented the taxable rating, but not the engine's true horsepower; "F" stood for foreign). Previously produced at the Trafford Park plant, the AF was very unpopular; according to Steven Tolliday, writing in "The Origins of Ford of Europe" (included in *Ford: 1903–2003: The European History, Volume I*), Dagenham only built five AFs but capitalized on commercial truck sales.

Ford quickly created the bantam-size four-passenger Model Y that had a 90-inch wheelbase and was 45 inches wide. The first in a line of cars that went by the names Popular, Prefect, Anglia, and others, the prototype "baby" Ford debuted in February 1932 in London. The car featured a 933-cc four-cylinder engine that was created by Laurence Sheldrick and produced an advertised 8 horsepower (the actual rating was 22 horsepower). The "Y" had a three-speed transmission, transverse leaf springs, and a Model T-like thermo-siphon cooling system that sucked coolant into the engine rather than using a water pump.

Coming in single-entrance and double-entrance saloon versions (i.e. two- and four-door sedans), the Model Y was a simple design with a starting price of £120. The car's fuel mileage was estimated around 43 miles per gallon, and its top speed was about 55 miles per hour.

The British Fords

Produced through the 1937 model year, the base Model Ys became known as the "Popular" in October 1935 when Perry dropped the base price for the two-door saloon to £100 and captured 54 percent of the British market. (All Populars were Model Ys, but not all Model Ys were Populars.) Competing against models from Austin, Hillman, Morris, and Singer, the Popular was the only fully equipped car at that price. In France, the "Y" was known as the Ford 6 CV where it was sold from 1932 to 1934; in Germany, it was called the Ford Köln and sold from 1933 to 1936. Ford had a knockdown assembly plant at Geelong, Victoria, Australia where a coupe version of the "Y" was sold with bodies designed by Lew Bandt, plus it was assembled in small numbers in Japan, Latvia—where it was called the Ford Junior—and Barcelona, Spain, as the Ford Modelo 8 (nicknamed the "Forito" or "little Ford").

In 1934, the Model Y engine was bumped up to 1,172 cc by increasing the cylinder bore from 56.6 millimeters (2.23 inches) to 63.5 millimeters (2.5 inches) but keeping the piston stroke at 92.5 millimeters (3.64 inches). Rated at 10 horsepower for

Eleven-year-old Henry Ford II sits atop a piling, flanked by his father, Edsel Ford, and Sir Percival Perry on May 16, 1929, for the Dagenham plant groundbreaking. As chairman of Ford of England, Perry envisioned Dagenham as a European Rouge producing 250,000 cars per year. *The Henry Ford*

tax purposes (the engine achieved 30 actual horsepower), this version was called the Model C (the CX by 1936)—also known as the Ford De Luxe Ten—that came in tourer, saloon, and luxury styles. Getting 35 miles per gallon, the car's top speed was 70 miles per hour. A tiny V-8 engine was initially planned for the car, but the motor was never put into production. The Model C was produced in Spain from 1934 until 1936; it was called the Ford Eifel in Germany and Hungary. Australia also started making the "C" in 1935 where it came in coupe, roadster, roadster utility, saloon, and van body styles.

The first Dagenham preproduction V-8s came off the line in March 1935 and four months later, in July, the first engine blocks came out of the factory's foundry. The first British production V-8 was completed on July 17, 1935. Prior to that time, all V-8 models and engines had been imported from Canada. The British V-8 bodies were again made by Briggs and were similar to those made in France.

By 1936, the "Ys" and Model CX took on a more semi-streamlined look and had larger bodies. Standard equipment included bumpers, direction indicators operated from the steering wheel (turn signals were often available as aftermarket accessories in America at this time), an indirectly lit instrument panel, twin windshield wipers, a rear window blind operated from the driver's seat, a foot control to dim the headlights, and an adjustable semi-bucket driver seat. Sliding roofs were available for an additional £6. The car had a durable cloth interior that matched the body color, but leather could be ordered for an extra £6. The touring car came with all-weather equipment and leather upholstery.

Ford of England's commercial vehicles in 1936 also included the three-wheel Tug, an 8-horsepower vehicle that was billed as the "mechanical horse." Sold at £215, the tug was designed for hauling trailers with a 2-ton payload over short distances in confined areas, but only about 120 units were built.

Between 1932 and 1937, Ford only sold 38,227 Model Ys on the European continent, roughly 6,000 cars a year, which was far below the 1930 revised target of 77,000 units annually. The De Luxe Ten's (Model C/CX) sales high point was 32,653 units in 1936 but plunged to 2,500 units in 1937. The "CX" was replaced by the Model 7W (known as the Ford Ten) that was soon superseded by the Prefect.

Coach Builders

Briggs supplied the regular Ford bodies for Dagenham, though its England plant lacked the presses to stamp out metal roof panels, so the Ford saloons featured a fabric-covered insert. Though there was the potential of leaks, the insert eliminated "body drumming," vibration noises that plagued many early closed cars. Other English Ford bodies were provided by coachbuilders, including Messrs. Dagenham Motors, Ltd.; W. Harold Perry, Ltd.; and W. J. Reynolds. Messrs. Knibbs and Parkyn did the coachwork on the larger Fords. As the 1930s progressed, the Fords received a semi-streamlined look.

When Edsel toured England in 1935, he met with the Jensen Brothers—Allan and Richard—who were coachbuilders for Singer, Standard, and Wolseley. Edsel commissioned them to build sportsters based on the Ford V-8.

From 1934 to 1937, S-Type Jensen Fords were equipped either with the 2.2-liter (135.9-cubic-inch) V-8-60 or 3.6-liter (221-cubic-inch) V-8-85 engines, plus twin downdraft carburetors, a Vertex ignition, and the Columbia two-speed rear axle. Many of the Jensen Fords were four-seat touring cars.

Ford's Dagenham plant sits along the River Thames in 1935. It had its own steel mills, one of the largest blast furnaces in Britain (producing 500 tons of pig iron a day), and an 1,800-foot-long jetty to handle oceangoing freighters. In 1936, a 170-foot-long, 60-foot-high "Ford" sign that was added to the powerhouse could be seen from miles away. *The Henry Ford*

The Ford Model Y, also called the Ford "baby" and later the Ford Eight, was a bantam-size British car with a four-cylinder engine that produced an advertised 8 horsepower (the actual rating was 22 horsepower). This was the first car designed by Bob Gregorie. This photo was taken on March 16, 1932, outside of the Engineering Laboratory Building in Dearborn. This is a prototype with more louvers than the production model. *The Henry Ford*

The new 10-horsepower Model C and the Model Y come off the same assembly line at Dagenham in 1934. The lighter cars are Ys painted in Electric Blue, which was only offered that model year. In 1935, Dagenham started producing its first V-8 engines instead of importing them from Canada. Also, the Model Y became known as the "Popular" when the base price for the two-door saloon dropped to £100. *The Henry Ford*

Other European coachbuilders made custom versions of the V-8 and English Fords. In Germany, the Eifel convertible cabriolet had cut-down doors and resembled a three-quarter-scale version of the 1935 American Ford. Custom or semi-custom bodies could be ordered from Kellner and Lagenthal and others.

Dagenham-produced trucks also varied from their American counterparts. For example, the Model 61 truck debuted in October 1935 and featured the 22–British horsepower V-8 engine (roughly a year before the V-8-60 arrived in the States), but it was not as popular a motor in England as the Ford Model Ten's four-cylinder.

The French Connection

By 1925, Ford was France's third-largest carmaker, behind Citroën and Renault, when it opened a new assembly plant at Asnières, near the outskirts of Paris, just before Model T sales plunged. In 1929, Ford of France underwent a restructuring, becoming Ford Société Anonyme Française, or Ford SAF for short.

With the onset of the Great Depression, the United States passed the Smoot-Hawley Tariff, a protectionist measure that raised the importation tax to one of the highest levels in American history. In retaliation, France in 1930 raised *its* tariffs,

imposing a 70 percent ad valorem tax on foreign finished cars and a 90 to 150 percent duty on imported components.

Under managing director Maurice Dollfus of Paris, Ford SAF went upmarket, stressing the luxury qualities of the Ford V-8s. It virtually abandoned small cars for the higher-priced segment, which could absorb the heavy customs duties. Dollfus was a handsome financier, Edsel's friend, and a member of the board of the Spanish luxury carmaker Hispano-Suiza. He had many friends and contacts in the French government, banking, and industrial circles.

Dollfus convinced Ford's American executives to allow Ford SAF to partner with E.E.C. Mathis, the maker of a small, four-cylinder car. In 1934, Ford of England sold most of its stock in Ford SAF to its American parent to form a joint-venture firm called Matford SA.

Ford owned 60 percent of Matford and had a majority of the seats on the board of directors; Dollfus became the managing director. Incorporated on September 27, 1934, the company leased the Ford SAF plant at Asnières and the Mathis assembly plant at Strasbourg, even though Ford executive Charles Sorensen thought the Mathis factory was antiquated.

At first Matford produced both the Mathis and the Matford, a French version of the Ford V-8. In 1935, Dollfus persuaded the

The British Horsepower Tax

Some of the oddest sights to Americans traveling to Europe in the 1930s were the English cars with small chassis with short wheelbases but large bodies that made them seem top heavy. The cars were the result of England's horsepower and heavy-fuel taxes that favored cars that had tiny engines but were large enough to accommodate families. The horsepower tax was copied by Ireland and some other European countries.

English cars were designed for start-stop motoring with rapid acceleration and a high top speed for travel along narrow, winding roads. They were not built for sustained running on the then-new German autobahns (high-speed motorways), where cars could be driven at full throttle for many miles without stopping.

The British horsepower formula was similar to that used by the Society of Automotive Engineers (SAE) but used different calculations.

For tax purposes, it was based on the cubic capacity of the cylinders, resulting in smaller engines to develop high speeds and multi-ratio transmissions to provide flexibility and power. Ford's 85-horsepower V-8 was rated as having 30 horsepower for taxable purposes, while the "thrifty sixty" had a 21.63-horsepower rating (often rounded up to 22 in advertising).

At one point the tax was a flat pound Sterling per horsepower (about $4.75 per horsepower unit according to 1930s exchange rates). Two great classes of automobiles resulted: small, low-cost cars and luxury cars. During the 1930s, the British horsepower tax dipped to about £4 10s—the equivalent of about $21.50—for cars not exceeding a 6-horsepower rating. An additional 15 shillings was charged for each unit of rated horsepower above a six. Although still costly, when the tax dropped, the 10-horsepower cars became more popular.

In mid-1939, the British government suddenly announced that the horsepower tax would rise by 66 2/3 percent on January 1, 1940, making it the most severe in British history. At the exchange rates at that time, the tax would amount to $5.87 per horsepower unit, compared with the former rate of $3.52 per unit.

"Whether the increase was for revenue or to discourage the manufacture of passenger cars so that plants could be devoted to munitions production could not, of course, be ascertained," *Automobile Topics* reported in its May 1, 1939, issue. Also, British gasoline taxes were very high—making fuel prices the equivalent of 32 cents American per gallon versus 10 cents in the United States.

The British car industry anticipated the increased tax would hit the sales of its 10-horsepower and larger cars, but then World War II started and civilian car production soon ended.

board of directors to drop the Mathis marque and concentrate on the V-8s. Engines, transmissions, and rear axles were made in Strasbourg, while much of the bodywork came from French suppliers.

Matford advertisements stressed the V-8 as "the car of the future." The V-8 symbol, as it often did in American advertising, figured prominently. Other ads talked about the car as being "the very monument of mechanical power," having "the will of speed," epitomizing "the greatest thrill in motoring," or being "the summit of perfection." Beginning with the 1936 Matford Model 68, the French joint venture moved away from using the big American Fords in favor of a 108 1/2-inch wheelbase chassis, though it offered both the 60- and 85-horsepower engines in a variety of styles. Matford was the first to start using the 60-horsepower "Alsace" V-8s in the fall of 1935. Cars like the 1938 Matford Cabriolet were given unique body styles and different headlights that distinguished them from the American-made Fords.

In October 1935 Italy invaded Ethiopia, while in 1936 the Spanish Civil War broke out and Germany reoccupied the Rhineland. When French troop trains, machine guns, and artillery units were stationed in Strasbourg, Dollfus began looking for a new production site.

A National Asset

Ford opened its first German branch assembly plant in Berlin in 1926. Percival Perry wanted to expand Ford Werke, as the subsidiary was called, as the largest of the continental companies. When Henry Ford visited Europe in autumn 1930, he laid the cornerstone for a new factory in Cologne and was lauded as "the American automobile king." Built on 52 acres along the bank of the Rhine River, the Cologne plant opened in June 1931 amid dismal economic conditions.

In the 1932 election, the Nazis became the largest party in the Reichstag (the German parliament) by promising to restore national pride, abrogate the humiliating Versailles

The Matfords retained the vertical, V-shaped front grilles that looked similar to the 1937 Fords, and had smaller bodies and other distinct features, such as the shape of the headlights and taillamps. This car has a leather interior and an armrest for the rear bench seat. *National Automotive History Collection, Detroit Public Library*

The year of this Matford Convertible Coupe is unidentified on the photograph, but it appears to have a "banjo" type steering wheel similar to the 1938 Ford De Luxe. This car is equipped with whitewall tires, a trunk-mounted spare tire, a V windshield, dual sun visors, and cowl-mounted dual wipers. The dual taillights jut out rather than being integrated into the fenders as on an American car. *National Automotive History Collection, Detroit Public Library*

Treaty that ended World War I, and create full employment. The Nazis blamed Jews and Marxists for the country's failings. In January 1933, President Paul von Hindenburg appointed Adolf Hitler chancellor; the Nazi leader soon made a bid for greater power.

In late February 1933, 25-year-old Walter Reuther, fairly fresh from being fired from Ford's Highland Park plant, and his younger brother, Victor, arrived in their ancestral homeland, visiting unionists and distant relatives. The German visit was a stop along their journey to the city of Gorky, where the Russians needed American expertise to build Ford Model As at the new Soviet-Ford joint-venture plant. Three days after the Reuthers' arrival in Berlin, on the night of February 27, 1933, the Reichstag caught on fire.

"Brown-shirted storm troopers were everywhere," Victor Reuther recounted visiting Berlin shortly after the fire, "hawking special editions of the Nazi-controlled newspapers, which were promoting [Nazi propagandist Joseph] Goebbels'

fabrications about a Communist-Socialist plot to start a civil war."

The Reichstag gave Hitler dictatorial powers. Promising a "New Germany," Hitler recognized the automotive industry as a national asset. He once told a German on his way to America to visit the Rouge Plant, "I shall do my best to put [Henry Ford's] theories into practice in Germany. . . . I have come to the conclusion that the motor car, instead of being a class-dividing element, can be the instrument for uniting the different classes, just as it has done in America, thanks to Mr. Ford's genius."

Ford Werke in Hitler's New Germany

Ford Werke found little respite as the Third Reich imposed onerous restrictions on the automotive industry, including directives that required practically all components to be made in Germany from German materials. All cars had to have standard parts that were interchangeable from one German company to the next.

While GM's wholly owned Adam Opel company quickly met the directives, Ford initially resisted the order to make its parts interchangeable with other German cars, arguing that it would destroy its German cars' parts interchangeability with other Ford products.

Ford's first car with a German name was the Köln (the British Model Y). In 1933, Ford Werke manager Edmund C. Heine wanted to place the words *Deutsches Erzeugnis* (made in Germany) on the Köln's hood, but the government stopped the plan when it discovered that only 50 percent of the cars' parts were actually made in the country. The Eifel (the British Models C and CX) was introduced to Germany while the American Model B was rebadged as the Rhineland and sold along with the Ford V-8. On June 16, 1935, Ford Werke manufactured its first German-made V-8 engine. The Ford emblem was still present on the cars but in a subtle form.

Despite its successes, Ford Werke's financial condition deteriorated. The Nazis didn't like Heine, a naturalized American citizen, because he had immigrated to the United States before World War I. They accused him of making munitions against his homeland during the war and then returning to German as an overlord after "making it big."

When auditors found that Ford Werke suffered from "loose management and supervision," Heine resigned on May 28, 1935. To replace him, Dr. Heinrich F. Albert, one of the most powerful members of the Ford Werke board of directors and former ambassador to the United States, helped choose Erick Diestel, the former manager of Berlin Electric Works. Diestel was a curious choice because he had little experience with car manufacturing or sales. In fact, it was said that Diestel never owned a car and could not drive.

Rehabilitating the company, Diestel made sure that by 1936 no Ford Werke–produced car exceeded the official limit of 5 percent foreign parts. To meet the Third Reich's demands to expand German exports, Diestel convinced Perry to open Denmark, Romania, Bulgaria, and central Europe—regions that were Dagenham's exclusive selling territory—to Cologne-produced cars. Ford Werke also supplied Ford's Portuguese company, which in turn sold to General Francisco Franco's forces during the Spanish Civil War. In exchange for growing its exports, the German government allowed Ford Werke to import much needed iron, copper, and rubber supplies.

Ford Werke received a boost on February 15, 1936, when Hitler and top Nazi officials visited the Ford display during the

After France raised its import tariffs during the Great Depression, Ford of France and Mathis created a joint-venture company in 1934 called Matford. Shortly thereafter, the four-cylinder Mathis car was discontinued as the company concentrated on producing V-8s under the Matford name. This is the exterior of the Mathis plant in Strasbourg, France, near the German border. *The Henry Ford*

This car comprises a 1937 Ford Köln cabriolet body mounted on an English Model C chassis and an eclectic mix of components from different model years. More German-made Fords, some finished and others unfinished, are visible in the background. *The Henry Ford*

opening ceremonies of International Automobile Exposition in Berlin. Writing to Sorensen, Diestel gushed that the company's display was placed in the middle of the hall as opposed to being shoved off to the side.

"You are no doubt aware that Herr Hitler is highly interested in the automobile industry; thus he also stayed at our stand for a while and I took the opportunity of a short discussion with him in regard to our production," Diestel wrote in a letter now in the collections of The Henry Ford. "It was not less remarkable that Herr Hitler, in his opening speech, mentioned Ford as the pioneer for the automobile as a means of transportation for the masses and that he recommended those principals on which the Ford enterprise is based, to be followed and imitated by the German Automobile Industry."

With the favorable reaction from the Führer, Ford's German dealers ordered 2,100 units—800 trucks, 500 V-8s, and 600 Eifels—the most at any one time in Ford Werke's history.

Proving Its German Character

Ford's cause in Germany was supported by Prince Louis Ferdinand of Prussia, who had befriended Henry Ford when

he worked for the automaker in Detroit from 1929 to 1934. Ferdinand became linked to German resistance groups and had connections to the German officers who unsuccessfully plotted to assassinate Hitler in 1944, Eric Pace noted in his 1994 *New York Times* obituary of Ferdinand.

In 1936, Dr. Albert acquiesced to the Nazi requirements that Ford parts should be interchangeable with other German vehicles. After learning that Diestel had Jewish ancestry, Albert attempted to fire him. Intervening, Sorensen said Diestel had a good grasp of Ford's operations and that Albert was "too impressed with the necessity of cooperating with German authorities."

In another effort to prove its German character, Ford Werke designed a new logo for its cars showing the Cologne plant and the city's landmark cathedral. As Paul Thomes wrote in *Ford: The European History, Volume II*, the Ford oval was reserved only for cars imported from the United States. Given Nazi import restrictions, those numbers were negligible.

In January 1937, the Third Reich permitted Ford Werke to bid for government contracts. According to Hubert Bonin in *Ford: The European History, Volume I*, a German executive commented, "according to present German ideas, an enterprise in Germany is only justified to exist in so far as it submits to the general political and economic requirements of the state."

That same year, Albert became chairman of the subsidiary's board of directors when Perry resigned to concentrate more on Ford of England. In 1938, Diestel negotiated with the Wehrmacht (Germany army) to assemble a military truck capable of carrying 3 tons across muddy and broken terrain. Henry and Edsel Ford rejected the war truck, but the German executives had their own plans. In April 1938, Ford Werke's directors approved a joint-venture plan with Ambi-Budd to acquire an assembly plant near Berlin purportedly to build ordinary trucks and V-8 passenger cars. The Nazi government then ordered 3,150 trucks plus passenger car chassis to be delivered by March 1939.

Diestel's management style—in which he ignored Ford directives and clashed with Albert—drew criticism from

Henry Ford laid the cornerstone for Germany's Cologne assembly plant on the Rhine River in the autumn of 1930, about a year after British troops (who had been stationed in the city since the end of World War I) had withdrawn. The Cologne plant opened in 1931 just before Adolf Hitler rose to power. *The Henry Ford*

Two unidentified Ford Werke executives stand with the first V-8 engine produced in Cologne in 1935. The Nazi government required practically all car components to be made in Germany from German materials. *The Henry Ford*

Above: Rows of V-8 engines, mated to their transmissions, are tested at Ford Werke's Cologne plant. Connected to an electrical source, the motors are revved to their highest level to check their performance before they are mounted in vehicles. *The Henry Ford*

Left: Ford Werke received a boost to its "Germanness" on February 15, 1936, when Chancellor Adolph Hitler and other top Nazi officials visited the Ford stand during the opening ceremonies of International Automobile Exposition in Berlin. Hitler is looking at a Ford V-8 limousine, which was one of eight-passenger cars equipped with bodies from German custom body makers. *The Henry Ford*

Sorensen and Perry. In November 1938, Albert traveled to Dearborn to meet with Edsel Ford, Perry (who had become "Lord Perry of Stock Harvard"), and Sorensen. They unanimously decided Diestel had to leave. After hearing of their decision, Diestel resigned in December 1938. He was replaced by Ford purchasing executive Robert Schmidt, even though Sorensen had deep reservations about Schmidt's capabilities.

"Worker's Paradise"

Ford's joint-venture plant with the Soviet Union was located in Gorky (which had been known as Novgorod until it was renamed in 1932), about 250 miles northeast of Moscow on the Volga River. Often called the gateway to Siberia, Gorky became the "Soviet Detroit" as it was turned into a military-industrial and research center. Victor Reuther noted with irony that Henry Ford was "quite willing to deal with real Bolsheviks—for cash on the line" rather than with American labor unions during the 1930s. Besides Victor and Walter Reuther, a number of Americans took their families to work at Ford's Model A and tractor factories in Gorky. At the time, Russia was actively luring thousands of Americans to their country to pass on their knowledge and skills, but also confiscating their passports and, in some cases, fraudulently getting them to sign forms to become Soviet citizens. The Soviets courted Ford and many other American and European companies with promises of big profits—even as millions of people were starving to death because of Stalin's farm collectivization policies.

Initially the Soviets opted for building Model A passenger cars and Model AA trucks because the vehicles had a simpler engine and were more suited for their roads. They paid Ford $40 million in gold for tooling that the company was going to discard anyway.

When the first cars came off the line in 1933 under giant portraits of Josef Stalin, they were badged as GAZ-A (GAZ stood for Gorky Avto Zavod) and celebrated as achievements of Soviet engineering. In 1936, when most of the American workers—including the Reuther brothers—returned to the United States when their contracts expired, the Gorky plant began producing Model Bs, rebadged as the GAZ M-1 (the "M" stood for Molotov, after Soviet Foreign Minister Vyacheslav Molotov). The cars were two to six years behind American style and technology but would be produced for the Soviet military through World War II.

Ford Around the World

By the mid-1930s, Ford had captured one-third of the Spanish market; however, the Spanish Civil War erupted on July 18, 1936. In a prelude to World War II, the insurgents led by General Franco were supported by Hitler and Italy's Benito Mussolini; Stalin backed the Loyalist (socialist) side.

Deciding not to favor either side, Ford allowed its Barcelona plant to remain open—even though GM closed its plant there—and sold vehicles to the Loyalists. Meanwhile, Ford of England and Ford Werke supplied cars and trucks to Ford's Portuguese subsidiary, which, in turn, sold cars and spare parts to Franco.

Ford's "split the middle" policy in Spain generated a lot of ill will when Franco's forces won the war on April 1, 1939. While

This lineup depicts vehicles produced at the Soviet Union-Ford plant at the city of Gorky on April 23, 1935. The Soviets initially opted for building Model A passenger cars and Model AA trucks because the vehicles had simpler engines and were more suited for the nation's roads. Shown outside of the Gorky Avto Zavod's Pressed Steel Building are a pickup truck, a GAZ-A four-door phaeton-styled car, a truck, and a bus. *The Henry Ford*

About a dozen rolling truck chassis are visible along with several partially completed 1939 Fords and Lincoln K Models at the Singapore branch assembly plant. The Second Sino-Japanese War is raging, and within two years, the Empire of Japan will be at war with the United States and Great Britain. *The Henry Ford*

GM, Chrysler, and other American firms had allowed Franco to purchase goods on credit, Ford required him to pay cash and lost much of its market share in Franco's Spain.

Italy was another trouble spot for Ford. As part of its invasion needs for Ethiopia, the Italian military ordered 4,767 trucks from Ford's Egyptian company in 1935—a nearly 600 percent jump from Italy's 1934 purchase of 802 trucks. Following reports that Italian troops used poison gas in Ethiopia, Henry Ford imposed his own embargo and canceled the remaining order of 800 trucks for the Italian army. Mussolini's government retaliated by imposing a 300 percent import duty on Ford cars, making the price five times the equivalent of a similar model in the United States. Perry reduced Ford's operations there to a bare minimum.

Ford of Canada was a major supplier of automobile parts and cars to distant parts of the British Empire and other areas from harbors of the Dutch East Indies (modern Indonesia), British Guinea, British Borneo, and Fiji. Ford's Windsor,

A circa 1935 photo shows Model 46 V-8s and Model Ys (known as the Modelo 8) at Ford's Barcelona assembly plant. Visible are the body trim line, water sanding, and final hardware conveyors. Ford controlled one-third of the Spanish market before the country plunged into civil war. *The Henry Ford*

Ontario, plant employed 7,000 to 8,000 workers who made 70,000 to 80,000 vehicles annually—many of them American designs with Canadian content—and supplied satellite assembly plants in South Africa, Australia, India, Malaya, New Zealand, and Singapore.

In Central and South America, Ford supplied mostly American- and British-designed cars, though German-made Fords were also sold in countries such as Brazil and Argentina.

Some of the rubber used to make Ford tires at the Rouge originated from Ford-owned lands in Brazil. In the mid-1920s amid soaring raw rubber prices, Ford purchased 2.5 million acres on the Tapajos River, a tributary of the Amazon, to start a rubber plantation called Fordlandia. The company built railroads, airports, schools, banks, houses, and a hospital, but the Depression cut the demand for cars and thus tires. The first rubber trees only started maturing by the late 1930s, and Ford had to import most of its rubber from the British East Indies. During World War II, synthetic rubber became the norm for

Three Ford Werke—built Eifels are displayed at a dealer showroom in Sao Paulo, Brazil. To meet Nazi Germany's demands to expand exports, Ford Werke managers convinced Percival Perry to open up regions that had been Dagenham's exclusive selling territory to Cologne-produced cars. *The Henry Ford*

The assistant manager of Ford's Copenhagen plant delivers a 1939 Mercury Town Sedan to their royal highnesses Prince Knud and Princess Caroline Mathilde of Denmark. This photo was published in the September 1939 issue of *Ford News*, just as World War II broke out with the German and Soviet Union invasions of Poland. On April 9, 1940, Germany invaded Denmark, purportedly to preempt a British invasion. *The Henry Ford*

he 1937 Model 7Y was Ford's first car designed and developed in the United Kingdom by Briggs. Basically a reworked Model Y, it used Model CX brakes, wheels, and steering components, and added four rubber engine-mounting points to reduce motor vibration. *The Henry Ford*

driver takes his English-built 1939 Ford V-8 "30" Convertible Coupe out for a countryside drive. The car comes complete with a rumble seat. Although the British rating for this car was 30 horsepower for axable purposes, it is equipped with the 85-horsepower flathead engine. *Detroit Public Library, National Automotive History Collection*

It can be yours -

THE £100 FORD SALOON

The 8-horsepower Ford Model Y was renamed the Popular in 1935 when its price was lowered to £100. It was the lowest-priced fully equipped saloon car ever made. *Detroit Public Library, National Automotive History Collection*

tire making. Ultimately, the Brazil venture racked up $20 million in losses and was sold off in 1945.

In Japan, where Ford's branch assembly plant used knockdown components from the Rouge and Canada, sales were hampered by Japanese trade restrictions designed to protect Nissan and Toyota. The Second Sino-Japanese War further depressed Ford's sales efforts.

The First English-Designed Ford

After the introduction of the Model C, Edsel Ford asked Sir Percival Perry to drop the Model Y and concentrate on the larger car. Knowing his market better than the executives in Dearborn, Perry refused. In 1937, Ford of England debuted the 1938 Model 7Y (the Ford Eight) and the 7W (the Ford Ten that replaced the De Luxe). The 7Y was the first Ford designed and developed in the United Kingdom by Briggs. Basically a reworked Popular, it used Model CX brakes, wheels, and

steering components, and added four rubber engine-mounting points to reduce motor vibration. Like the V-8s, the new Popular had an enclosed trunk (or "boot") and a wide choice of all-steel body styles similar to the larger streamlined V-8s. Standard equipment included safety glass, pressed-steel wheels, dual wipers, turn signals, front and rear bumpers, a 6 1/2-gallon fuel tank, interior light, and a rear window blind. A sliding roof was optional and the cars came in two- or four-door saloon models. The 7W was 2 1/2 inches longer and 3 inches wider than the Ford Eight; it also came in an open touring model with leather upholstery.

Although one of Ford's most successful car lines in the late 1930s, the 7Y/7W was almost canceled because Sorensen didn't like the design. When he saw the prototypes, Sorensen told the Dagenham managers to "take an ax and chop them up." According to David Burgess-Wise, in his book, *Ford at Dagenham*, Irish-born executive Patrick Hennessy traveled to

Dearborn and received Henry's blessing for the 7Y project after a game of baseball with schoolchildren at Greenfield Village.

Using the "Y" chassis, Dagenham also created the small Model 7Y truck and the Model E83W, a half-ton, cab-over-engine design with the 10-horsepower engine. In 1938, Ford of England's American parent bowed to buyer pressure and allowed Ford of Britain to offer trucks with an optional four-cylinder.

The V-8 was overpowered for England's road conditions. Trucks often had to drive in low gear, resulting in heavy fuel consumption and excessive engine wear. After Ford had dropped its four-cylinder trucks in 1935, its market share dipped from 25 to 15 percent within a year while competitors Morris and

Bedford reaped the benefits. The 1937 Ford V-8s sold in the United Kingdom and Ireland were equipped with the 22– or 30–British horsepower engines (i.e., the V-8-60 and the V-8-85); some 2,796 and 3,805 units were produced, respectively. The 22-horsepower V-8 engine was also offered on a car with a 108 1/2-inch wheelbase. Very similar to the larger and heavier 112-inch-wheelbase model, the smaller Ford had a flat windshield instead of a V-shape, plus the headlights were mounted in separate pods rather than being recessed into the fenders. Starting prices were £230 for the Standard Fordor Ford and £240 for the De Luxe Fordor and Touring cars.

Giving a European perspective, *The Irish Motor News* said that the Ford V-8s were reliable, could handle "atrocious road

This is a Cologne-produced Model C delivery van from 1937. The body was 100 inches long, 56 inches wide, and 51 inches tall. The van had a total carry capacity of 250 kilograms. *The Henry Ford*

V8

F 82 A

CONDUITE INTÉRIEURE
TOURISME GRAND LUXE

Vue arrière de la Conduite Intérieure Luxe.

Vue arrière de la Conduite Intérieure
Tourisme Grand Luxe.

CONDUITE INTÉRIEURE LUXE

CABRIOLET 5 PLACES

Cabriolet 5 places, en milord.

Cabriolet 5 places, décapoté.

A sales brochure shows the range of the 1938 Matford F82 A luxury saloon and cabriolet models. The cars could be ordered with or without a trunk. *Michael W. MacSems collection.*

surfaces, often under adverse conditions," and had "fine braking and faultless handling. . . . The all-around excellence of the Ford V-8 cannot be overlooked or explained away."

Depression Returns

Concurrent with America's falling economy in 1938, the Depression returned in Europe. To make matters worse for Ford of England, there was a sudden rush of cheap imported German cars—mostly Opels—that undersold British models. Percival Perry accused the German government of subsidizing the exports.

That fall, Ford of Britain introduced the Prefect, a reworking of the Model 7W. Called the Prefect because it was "at the head of its class," according to advertisements, the car's body styles included two- and four-door saloons, a tourer, and a coupe. New rivals in the 10-horsepower segment came from Hillman Standard Motor Company and GM's Vauxhall. Ford sold 14,453 Prefects its first year and 36,600 units in 1939, but output plunged to 9,924 in 1940 before civilian car production halted.

At Dagenham, total production fell from 77,830 units in 1937 to 59,935 units in 1938, of which 1,786 were the 30-horsepower V-8s, 2,200 were 22-horsepower V-8s, 28,000 were Model 7Ys, and 18,665 were Model 7Ws. The remainder were Prefects.

As war with Germany appeared more likely, Perry accepted a British government proposal to construct a "shadow plant" for defense purposes.

The Matford Partnership Unravels

In France, Matford faced continuing accusations from the French Automobile Employers' Association that it was not actually a French company because it used Ford's American design, engineering, and tooling resources. Émil Mathis grew disenchanted as managing director Maurice Dollfus and Ford SAF took more and more control of Matford. The joint venture began unraveling.

From Dollfus' perspective in mid-1937, the city of Strasbourg looked increasingly unsafe for an automobile

Ford SAF's new Poissy Plant, just outside of Paris, was still under construction on January 1, 1940, even as the company was attempting to fill orders for the French army and air force. Conceived of in 1937 by executive Maurice Dollfus, Poissy was supposed to become Ford SAF's premier assembly plant, able to produce 150 cars a day. *The Henry Ford*

assembly plant, especially with German troops just across the Rhine. When it came to Mathis, Dollfus felt that since Ford SAF had invested far more heavily into Matford, he had the right to direct the joint venture.

On March 26, 1937, Matford's board of directors, including Edsel Ford and Sorensen, approved a proposal by Dollfus to find land for a new factory close to Paris that would replace both Asnières and Strasbourg. By December 1937, Dollfus announced that Matford would build a new $4 million factory on a 60-acre site on the Seine River near Poissy, about 15 miles from the center of Paris. The plan called for the first car to be assembled before May 1, 1940, the date when the leases on Matford's two assembly plants expired. Poissy would be partially running by the first quarter of 1939. Mathis sued for damages, claiming that his business had been injured; he soon realized, however, that the joint-venture agreement allowed Matford to leave Strasbourg in 1940.

Building Poissy, International Crisis

Dollfus wanted to begin manufacturing a four-cylinder vehicle at Poissy, but rejected a proposal that he should use the design of the new Ford Taunus (based on the Model 7W) in Germany. He wanted a car similar in body style to the Peugeot 202.

Other French automakers were troubled by the prospects of the new factory with its projected output of 150 cars a day from a single eight-hour shift. In July 1939, Citroën's president said he "was frightened by the prospect of seeing arriving on the market a bunch of little Fords."

Overshadowing Dollfus' plans were twin international crises in 1938: the German annexation of Austria on March 12 and Hitler's expansionist plans for the Sudetenland, a territory of Czechoslovakia. The Sudetenland crisis brought Europe to the brink of war until the Munich Agreement was negotiated among England, France, Germany, Czechoslovakia, and Italy. Signed on September 29, the deal transferred the Sudetenland to Germany. The false peace kept for nearly a year.

As tensions with Germany grew, the French minister of defense asked Dollfus to build military aircraft engines, which were in short supply. In March 1939, Dollfus discussed the French government's proposal with company executives. In mid-May, France ordered 1,200 Rolls-Royce aircraft motors in a contract worth one billion francs. Fordair, a wholly owned subsidiary of Ford SAF, was incorporated in June, and on August 28, 1939 (four days before the German invasion of Poland), Fordair bought a plant in the port city of Bordeaux.

When the German Wehrmacht poured into Poland on September 1, 1939, France ordered Matford to evacuate Strasbourg's operations to Bordeaux. For three months, supplies and workers were tied up conducting the move even as the company was supposed to be completing Poissy.

The French army and then the air ministry also placed orders for 3.5- and 5-ton trucks. Some of the war materiels were produced at Asnières and Poissy, which wasn't fully tooled up until April 1940. To meet its new government contracts, Ford shipped some of the automobile machinery out of Poissy soon after it had been installed and important pieces of equipment were lost for a time at various train depots in the chaos that soon enveloped France.

Schmidt's Schemes

Ford Werke's new manager, Robert Schmidt, dreamed of a unified Ford of Europe under his control. Described as ruthless and opportunistic, Schmidt pledged loyalty to both Ford and the Nazis, though Ford Motor Company no longer had control of Ford Werke. (In addition, there is no proof that Schmidt joined the Nazi Party.)

By the end of 1938, total German vehicle production had risen to 342,000 units annually—up from a dismal 52,000 units in 1932. Ford Werke was Germany's third largest automaker, with an 11 percent market share, and the second largest producer of trucks. But Ford Werke lagged far behind GM's Opel, which had a 40 percent share, and just behind Dampf-Kraft-Wagen (DKW), a German automaker that had a 15 percent share. On a per capita basis, there was one automobile for every 55 Germans (versus one to every five Americans). There was a demand for more passenger cars—that was the impetus for Hitler to start Volkswagen in 1937—but civilian automobile production shrank while truck orders grew, thanks to military purchases. Without the government's truck purchases, one company manager said, "Ford would have lost all its German investment as the subsidiary withered due to a lack of a market."

Ford Werke's newest car was the 1939 Taunus, based on the British Model 7W. Named after a mountain range, it was the first German Ford to have hydraulic brakes. Equipped with a four-cylinder, 1,172-cc (71.52-cubic-inch) engine mated to a three-speed manual transmission, it produced 34 horsepower at 4,250 rpm. The Taunus had a streamlined body with a 94.1-inch wheelbase and an overall length of 161.8 inches, and weighed 1,830 pounds. Ford produced few prewar Taunuses. German civilian car production ended in 1940 and civilian truck production fell off by February 1941.

Although officially going along with Henry Ford's pacifist approach, which barred Ford Werke from directly manufacturing armaments, Schmidt and Ford Werke Chairman Heinrich Albert went beyond merely cooperating with Hitler's regime. According to Ford Motor Company's "Ford-Werke Under the Nazi Regime" (2001), Nazi officials approached Schmidt in late 1939 to build munitions for the Wehrmacht. The meeting resulted in the Arendt Plan, named after German car supplier Walter Arendt. A shadow war plant was built in Cologne; Arendt owned 24 percent of the company, and Schmidt was identified as owning the remaining 76 percent, though he claimed that Albert promised to reimburse any losses.

DIE FORD-TAUNUS-MANNSCHAFT AUF DER GROSSGLOCKNERSTRASSE
WÄHREND DER ALPENFAHRT 1939.

The 1939 Ford Taunus team takes three cars up a mountain road as part of a publicity shot prior to the outbreak of World War II. *The Henry Ford*

It's 1940. The war is on, and Ford Werke's German managers are no longer taking orders from Dearborn, but Ford's German subsidiary still takes the time to run an advertisement celebrating its 10th anniversary on the Rhine River. *The Henry Ford*

Men inspect damage to Ford of England's Dagenham plant after it was bombed by the German Luftwaffe on July 25, 1941. After the war began, the plant's roof was painted to look like the surrounding marshland, and its skylights were blacked out. Nevertheless, German bombers first struck on September 7, 1940. In all, 200 bombs fell on Dagenham during the war. *The Henry Ford*

Ford's top executives in America never authorized the Arendt Plan. American managers were suspicious of what Ford Werke was doing. According to both Allan Nevins' and Frank Hill's *Ford: Decline and Rebirth* and Ford Motor Company's "Ford-Werke Under the Nazi Regime," one engineer from Dearborn, Valentine Tallberg, tried to visit the Ford Werke-Ambi-Budd Berlin factory in 1939 but was refused admission because he was a foreigner. Even Robert Roberge, the Ford executive from Michigan who handled exports, had trouble entering the factory and could not find out what was being made there. What was produced there before the Ford Werke-Ambi-Budd joint venture ended in October 1941 were 1,838 SPKW (Schwerer Personenkraftwagen) armored personnel carriers. Ford's American executives were also unaware of the Cologne munitions plant.

The Berlin and Cologne plants produced 3-ton V-8-powered trucks for the German military and later the Maultier (Mule)

half-track personnel carrier. Once the war started in Europe, Ford Motor Company's contacts with Ford Werke and its operations in occupied Europe became sketchier and more infrequent. The Germans no longer took orders from Dearborn.

Ford: Axis and Allies

Before Winston Churchill became British prime minister in May 1940, Dagenham continued peacetime production with the launching of the Anglia, the successor to the Model 7Y. Only 5,136 Anglias were made before all civilian British production ended in 1941.

France's strategy was to fight a defensive war on the Western Front. Meanwhile, Ford SAF redesigned its trucks to a COE configuration to meet new French air ministry requirements.

Canada and other parts of the British Commonwealth joined the fight against Germany. Ford's Windsor assembly and the Toronto branch plant, like Dagenham in England, switched to war production. Limited civilian manufacturing continued at Windsor until March 31, 1942.

On May 9, 1940, German troops marched into Belgium, Holland, and Luxembourg. Less than a month later, on June 3, the Luftwaffe bombed Poissy but caused little damage. On June 10, as German troops advanced into France, the French government ordered Ford SAF to retreat and ship whatever it could from Poissy and Asnières to Bordeaux. France surrendered on June 22.

Ford SAF managing director Dollfus found himself in German-occupied Bordeaux. Upon returning to Paris, he discovered Schmidt and other Ford Werke executives were reorganizing the company. Asnières was placed under the control of Heinrich Albert, son of the Ford Werke chairman and would be sold off; Bordeaux would build aircraft components while Poissy would manufacture military trucks and engines.

As Dollfus got back to work as an executive at Ford SAF, there ensued a power struggle among him, Schmidt, and a German industrial consultant named Stahlberg who wanted administrative and managerial powers over Ford SAF. Dollfus

obtained a measure of autonomy in running the Poissy plant but bowed to German control. (Matford was formally dissolved in 1941 at the Nazis' insistence.) Since it was an important Axis manufactur, the British Royal Air Force heavily bombed Poissy in March and April 1942.

In England, Dagenham's roof was painted to look like the surrounding marshland and its skylights were blacked out, but it had little effect. German bombers first struck the plant on September 7, 1940, followed by raids on September 8 and again 10 days later. All in all, Dagenham was struck by 200 bombs during the war plus near misses from German V1 and V2 rockets.

By April 1941, Schmidt was appointed *wehrwirtschaftsführer* (war business leader) for the Cologne plant and Ford's subsidiaries in the Axis-occupied countries, which included at various times the Netherlands, Belgium, France, Luxemburg, Holland, Denmark, Italy, Hungary, Romania, and Finland. After Germany and Italy declared war on the United States, following the Japanese attack on Pearl Harbor, Schmidt's power at Ford Werke grew while Albert's declined. The Nazis learned that Albert had helped several Czechoslovakian Jews save some

Ford Werke's Berlin and Cologne plants produced 3-ton, V-8 powered trucks for the German military during the war. Nearly completed trucks are parked under a camouflage canopy in 1944. Ford Werke also made the Maultier, a half-track personnel carrier. *The Henry Ford*

This drawing shows the two-door saloon version of the Ford Prefect. Ford sold 14,453 Prefects in 1938 and 36,600 units in 1939, but output plunged to 9,924 units in 1940 before civilian car production halted during the war. *Detroit Public Library, National Automotive History Collection*

This is a 1939 Ford Köln V-8 Tudor Sedan. By the late 1930s, Ford Werke was Germany's fourth largest automaker, with an 11 percent market share, and the second largest producer of trucks. Although there was a demand in Germany for more passenger cars, civilian automobile production shrank as military orders grew. *The Henry Ford*

A group of French prisoners of war stands in front of a barracks at the Ford Werke plant in Cologne, circa 1943. This is one of three known photographs of the forced workers at Ford Werke during World War II. The overall numbers of forced/slave laborers at Cologne ranged from about 300 in 1942 to almost 2,000 by August 1944 and included Russians, Ukrainians, and Jews. *The Henry Ford*

of their property and that he had Jewish friends. Later, in September 1944, the Gestapo arrested Albert and held him for six months on the suspicion that he was involved with the July 20, 1944, assassination attempt on Hitler.

Communications between Ford Motor Company and its German managers ceased in November 1941 and were nonexistent after Pearl Harbor. There is little evidence that any executives at Ford's other European subsidiaries acted as intermediaries between Dearborn and Germany any time between November 1941 and 1945. In May 1942, the Superior Court in Cologne declared Ford Werke to be under enemy influence; in 1943, under U.S. law, Ford recorded its German operations as a total loss.

Schmidt sent mechanics and skilled workers to the Eastern front lines to train soldiers to repair vehicles. Short of homefront workers as it sent its men to the front lines, Nazi Germany began using forced laborers in its factories. Cologne was no exception.

The first French prisoners of war and Italian political prisoners arrived in Cologne in September 1940. They were housed in barracks adjacent to the factory at a site that became known as the "Ford camp"—supervised by plant guards and the Gestapo—and worked more than 60 hours a week (Allied war workers often worked similarly long shifts, too, though work was not done under the threat of execution). The overall numbers of forced laborers used by Ford Werke is unknown, but at Cologne it ranged from about 300 in 1942 to almost 2,000 by August 1944. Among them were Russian and Ukrainian prisoners, including 900 to 1,200 women.

The Buchenwald concentration camp also used one of its satellite camps near Cologne to provide slave laborers to Ford Werke before setting up a satellite camp at the factory, which housed 50 to 115 Jewish slave laborers. (By contrast, the German automotive supplier Siemens employed some 50,000 workers against their wills; Volkswagen and Daimler-Benz also were large users of forced laborers.)

Schmidt's "Ford of Europe" reached an all-time-high production level in December 1943 when it made 2,950 3-ton trucks and 1,000 Maultiers. As the Allies advanced, resistance sabotage slowed manufacturing to 30 to 50 percent below the level demanded by the Nazi government.

Liberation

Poissy was liberated at the end of August 1944 though it suffered heavy damage. Dollfus was arrested for collaboration but was soon freed, claiming that Ford SAF was the hostage of Nazi Germany. Back in charge, he had Poissy running again to make trucks for the Allies and to repair U.S. Army tank engines. In October 1945, the Americans awarded Dollfus for "distinguished service as a producer who played a major role in the Allied victory."

From September 1939 to March 1945, Ford Werke produced between 87,000 to 92,000 vehicles, including several models of 3-ton trucks and the Maultier. The factory accounted for one-third of Germany's wartime truck production. The Cologne plant was bombed several times, on May 30 and 31, 1942, and again in August and October 1944.

Two men salvage parts from a destroyed truck inside the Cologne plant's bombed-out garage in May 1945. This damage was termed "superficial" in comparison to the city, which took heavy damage.
The Henry Ford

When it looked like the Nazis would lose the war, Schmidt delayed the movement of equipment into the German interior and held off destroying the Cologne plant.

In early March 1945, U.S. troops reached Cologne. The Ford factory was struck by artillery fire. Despite all of the attacks, the facility only suffered superficial damage, though much of the city was destroyed. Allied bombings had also struck the Cologne Labor Office, destroying the records of forced labor usage.

After the war, Schmidt and 39 other Ford Werke managers and employees were investigated by the de-Nazification committee. Schmidt was imprisoned between June 1945 and September 1945, but the committee cleared him and the others of any charges. He was later reemployed by Ford of Germany in 1950 as a technical supervisor.

Even as a major truck producer, Ford Werke's contributions to the Nazi war machine paled in comparison to Ford Motor Company's output for the Allies. Ford of England manufactured 30,000 Rolls-Royce Merlin V-12 engines for four-engine bombers (ironically the same engines that Henry Ford refused to build in America), plus 347,000 army trucks and 13,942 Bren gun carriers powered by V-8 engines. In the United States, Ford built 8,685 B-24 Liberator bombers, 2,718 tanks and tank destroyers, 277,896 jeeps, 12,500 armored cars, 93,217 trucks, 13,000 amphibious vehicles, 4,291 gliders, and more.

Between 1940 and 1945 Ford's Dagenham Plant produced thousands of aircraft engines, vans, four-wheel-drive trucks, and V-8 powered Bren gun carriers, the latter were light tracked vehicles used to transport troops and equipment and often mounted with a machine gun. Here the 10,000th Bren carrier produced at Dagenham undergoes testing. *Detroit Public Library, National Automotive History Collection*

Two men photographed in a scrap yard circa 1943 indicate that this wrecked '40 Ford will get a second life after its steel is recycled into war materiel for use in the Pacific Theater. *Motorbooks collection*

Chapter Six

Sand, Dirt, and White Lightning

By 1901, 38-year-old Henry Ford had attained some measure of fame in his hometown of Detroit, but his first car venture had flopped. To resurrect his ambitions, on October 10, 1901, Henry and his riding mechanic, Ed "Spider" Huff, went head to head with the industry's most famous manufacturer, Alexander Winton, in a race sponsored by the Detroit Driving Club in what is now Detroit's exclusive Grosse Pointe suburbs.

Winton's car broke down and Ford's lighter machine won, gaining him national fame. Today, Winton's name is largely forgotten, but Henry used the race and other racing promotions featuring drivers such as Barney Oldfield to boost his car enterprise (the strategy was used by other car companies and led to the adage "Win on Sunday, Sell on Monday"). As Ford concentrated on selling its Model Ts as cheaply as possible, racing became less and less important to the automaker—at least officially. Whenever Ford cars did well at races—such as 1933 when Fred Frame won the Elgin (Illinois) National Road Race in a Ford V-8, or the Gilmore Gold Cup race when 22 of the 26 entrants were Fords—the company advertised the accomplishments to make sure buyers equated racing success with dependability.

After World War I, Ford pulled out of automotive racing until the mid-1930s when race car–engine maker Harry Armenius Miller and entrepreneur Preston Tucker approached Edsel Ford with a proposal to use the new V-8 engine to power a fleet of 10 race cars in the 1935 Indianapolis 500. The goal was to sweep the race, bringing more fame to the Ford V-8s—and to Miller and Tucker too.

Edsel approved of the project, but it took a while to convince his father. The project got off to a late start in February 1938 with a crash construction program at the Rouge Plant. What emerged were streamlined, front-wheel-drive, rear-engine beauties with low-slung bodies. Their V-8 engines had a compression ratio of 9.5:1 and produced 150 horsepower at 5,000 rpm. However, only four cars were completed in time for the May 30 race, and there was little practice time for the drivers to discover the flaws in the design.

Ford invited a large contingent of dealers to the speedway, and there was much press coverage leading up to the race, but the project led to frayed nerves and bitter feelings between Henry and Edsel. Only on race day was the Miller-Fords' fatal flaw discovered. As part of its streamlined design, the cars'

exhaust pipes were built into the steel floor. During the race, the exhaust heat cooked the grease out of the nearby steering-gearbox, causing mechanical breakdowns for three of the cars while the fourth succumbed to failure of its front-wheel-drive housing, again because of the heat. Ford did not return as an official race sponsor for 19 years. Henry confiscated the Miller-Ford cars but later sold them off to a group that included automotive supplier and former Ford employee Louis W. "Lew" Welch. A friend of Ford executive Ray Dahlinger, Welch resurrected the cars as the Novis, which achieved some measure of racing fame.

Although the company did not openly sponsor race cars, there were some rumors that Henry did financially back Welch and others in their racing endeavors. If the cars failed to perform, it would not hurt the company's reputation, but the automaker could still play up any wins in its advertising.

Europe's Greatest Race

One of Ford's greatest racing victories before the war was the 1938 Monte Carlo Rally in January when five Ford cars finished in the top seven: first place and places four through seven. Two other cars came in 14th and 15th. In all, 26 Fords had started the race; 25 of them were V-8s, and 19 had won one cup or another.

Unlike most American races, Monte Carlo was a test of driving skill over long distances in winter conditions. The starting points were Athens; Berlin; northern Scotland; Lisbon; Stavanger, Norway; Tallinn, Estonia; and Umea, Sweden. The routes across the Balkans, for example, were little more than unmarked tracks. Roads featured mud, snow, and cobblestones, and drivers needed boards, shovels, rope, and other paraphernalia to get through. Those who took the longest, most difficult roads on their way to Monaco received bonuses.

If the cars reached the checkpoints on time, the route to Monte Carlo became an elimination test. First place in 1938 was

Facing: Bob Rounthwaite, behind the wheel of No. 46A, turned 118.47 miles per hour at El Mirage Dry Lake in his flathead-powered '40 Tudor in 1950. *NHRA Museum*

133

taken by G. Bakker Schut and Klaas Barendrecht of Holland, who followed one of the most difficult routes from Athens north through Central Europe, and south over torturous Alpine roads. In another case, one driver and mechanic were ramming their Ford through snowdrifts in Lithuania when something pierced the gas tank. They had no choice but to continue slewing and skidding for 300 more miles before they could make repairs. Meanwhile, the mechanic ran a hose from the carburetor through a hole he had punched in the dashboard to the cabin, where he fed the carburetor fuel from a can. That team came in fourth.

Ford had also met with previous Monte Carlo success in 1936 when 26 Fords started and 16 finished, taking first, fourth, sixth, and ninth places.

Another Ford European victory was realized when a specially built Matford equipped with an 85-horsepower V-8 engine set 25 new world and international time and distance records in a 10-day continuous run in France from May 19 to 28, 1937. Officiated by the International Association of

Recognized Automobile Clubs, the races were conducted at the Montlhéry Autodrome near Paris. Four French women led by Mariette-Hélène Delangle, one of France's most celebrated drivers and a pioneer woman driver on the Grand Prix circuit, drove the Matford night and day. The car—nicknamed "Claire" in honor of teammate Claire Descollas who was forced to withdraw—averaged speeds of 140 to 144 kilometers per hour (86.9 to 89.4 miles per hour) and covered a distance of more than 32,000 kilometers (19,884 miles). The women set 10 world and 15 international Class C records, including driving 20,000 kilometers in 229 hours and 37 minutes at an average speed of 87.1 miles per hour. The previous record was 83.67 miles per hour.

The Gran Premio Nacional
South America also had a growing interest in auto racing during the late 1930s and Fords were prominently represented. The Gran Premio Nacional helped to spark a decades-long battle between "Fordistas" and "Chevroletistas" (Ford and Chevy

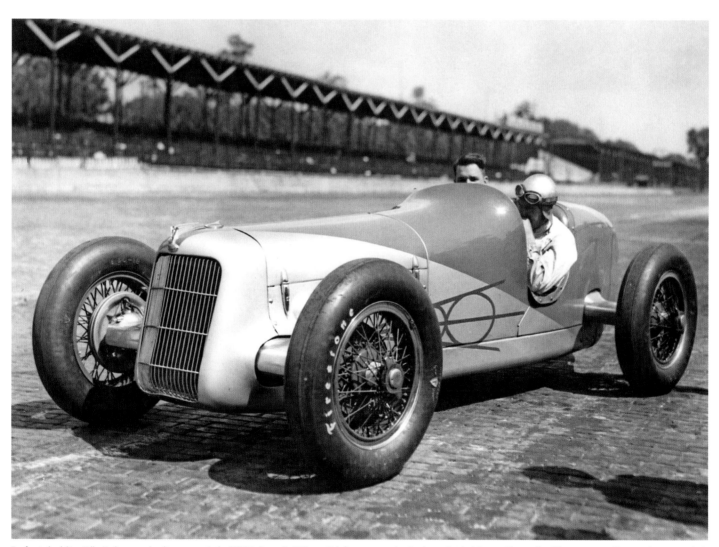

Ten front-wheel-drive Miller-Fords were ordered to compete in the 1935 Indianapolis 500 race. Only four were completed and none finished the race. Three suffered from steering problems, and one succumbed to a drivetrain failure due to the heat from the exhaust pipes. *The Henry Ford*

This Turismo Carretera (road racing) car was campaigned in one of the Argentinian Gran Premio Nacionals of the late 1930s. *The Henry Ford*

fans). The race—essentially Argentina's Grand Prize Race or Gran Prix—was a grueling multiday competition among stock American and European-built cars over 4,500-plus miles of rough roads.

One hundred and twenty-three cars started the 1938 race one minute after midnight in the rain in Buenos Aires on October 18. Twelve days later, after driving 4,565 miles at an average speed of 51.3 miles per hour, Ricardo Risatti and his companion sped over the finish line in their 1938 Ford Standard—sans the front and rear fenders and running boards. The race had been run in 10 stages through 14 Argentine provinces from the Atlantic seacoast to the Bolivian border and up the steep Andes Mountains. Torrential rains slowed the early part of the race. Only 22 cars finished the race; 15 of them were Fords. (Risatti had been racing to raise money to take his wife to Lourdes, France, but was unable to do so before she died.)

Finishing second was Angel Lo Valvo, who won the 1937 race in a Ford. Also participating in his first race was Oscar Galvez—driving a 1935 Ford—who became one of South American motorsports' leading champions.

By the end of 1938, Oscar's younger brother Juan was acting as his co-driver. The brothers were two of the fastest drivers in the world and ushered in a number of racing innovations, including installing oversized radiators to correct engine overheating problems and using a bottle behind the seat and a long straw to sip water without removing their hands from the wheel in 100-plus-degree Fahrenheit temperatures.

Oscar Galvez was declared the winner of the 1939 Gran Premio, which was stopped after 850 miles due to torrential rains. However, when the course dried out nine days later, the race proceeded under a different name, and Oscar won again over the 2,700-mile course.

A 1936 Ford Werke—built V-8 climbs a mountain road. The original caption to this picture noted, "Ford continues this year's series of successes on the International Alps Race." *The Henry Ford*

The Last Race

On September 9, 1939, the Irish Motor Racing Club sponsored "The Last Motor Race in Europe" before the end of the war, despite the onset of fuel rationing. "The threat, and later the onset, of war caused many car and motorcycle race meetings to be abandoned . . . until at last the only one left was the Irish Motor Racing Club's Phoenix Park races," noted The Irish Motor News in its September 21, 1939, issue.

One of these races was scratched due to a lack of participants—eight English drivers couldn't ship their cars to Ireland. Many drivers were enthusiasts who were unable to purchase "real" race cars due to heavy import duties, so they built their own stock car speed machines.

One of the biggest and fastest of the Irish cars of the era was the McQuillan-V-8-Special, owned by W. A. McQuillan. Originally a 1932 Grand Prix Bugatti, the two-seat car was outfitted with a modified Ford V-8 engine that achieved a

6.7:1 compression ratio and had a three-speed Ford gearbox. The car's maximum speed was more than 100 miles per hour. Yet McQuillan's car often suffered from various mechanical problems, and its performance at "The Last Race in Europe" was no exception.

Only 15 of 21 drivers were able to participate in 1939 Phoenix Park race in Dublin. After recording an 81.6-mile-per-hour lap from a standing stop and a flying lap at 85.2 miles per hour, the McQuillan car withdrew with black smoke issuing from under the hood due to a defective piston. The top cars included an N-type MG driven by P. M. Cahill and a supercharged M. G. Magnette with A. P. Macarthur behind the wheel.

The winner was the homemade Thompson-Racing-Special, which was a modified 1937 Ford Popular. Owned by Aubrey J. Thompson of Mallow, Cork County (the ancestral home of

Henry Ford's family), the car's chassis had been reinforced and lowered 4 inches. It was equipped with semi-independent front suspension and finished off with a radiator from a Ford Ten. Like the California dry lakes racers and the bootleggers in the South, Thompson had worked on other engine modifications, raising the four-cylinder's engine compression to 8:1 and installing a lighter flywheel, a de Dion–type rear suspension, and altered camshafts so four Amal motorcycle-type carburetors could be installed.

The TRS made a steady pace of about 83.8 miles per hour per lap, and cruised to home when Cahill's MG suffered clutch problems and a bad pit stop. Cahill settled for third place as Macarthur cruised into second place. Only three other cars completed the course. There were "no accidents of any kind to mar a pleasant afternoon's racing that would have been even more enjoyable in normal times," concluded The Irish Motor News.

In the 1940 Gran Premio, 110 cars started from Buenos Aires on the 850-mile-long leg to Tucuman in the foothills of the Catamarcan Precordillera. Passing into the mountains and through Bolivia's 15,000-foot passes, they went to La Paz, west to Peru, and up to Lima. Turning around, they raced back to Buenos Aires, with the finishers completing a 5,900-mile-long roundtrip. The winner of that race was Juan Manuel Fangio, who had been working in a Ford garage in Balcarce, but Fangio was driving a new Chevrolet coupe, not a Ford V-8. When the time came for Fangio to race, the Ford dealership didn't have a car available, but a Chevy was found at a nearby showroom. GM's Argentine managers took notice of the win, and the Ford-Chevy racing rivalry in South America was born.

On the Beach

The birth of a national motorsports empire began with the seemingly inconsequential decision by a family of three to take their $100 in savings and leave the Washington, D.C., area in 1934 and head south. "I started thinking if I was going to have to work all the time fixing automobiles, I might as well fix them where it wasn't snowing," William Henry Getty France told Sylvia Wilkinson in *Dirt Tracks to Glory*, a history of stock car racing's early days.

The racing bug had bitten France early. He had participated in a number of unsanctioned races, learning the hard way that the advertised prize money wasn't necessarily true. By the time he reached Daytona Beach, Florida, he ran out of money and his family settled there. Working as a gas station attendant, he fished and hunted rabbits to supplement his family's meals.

Daytona had been the scene of speed racing since the early 1900s, but the last race was held in 1935 when Sir Malcolm Campbell of Britain set a land speed record of 276 miles per hour in his Rolls-Royce–powered *Bluebird*. Afterward, the land speed races shifted to the more reliably flat Bonneville Salt Flats of Utah. To replace it, Daytona's civic leaders developed an 80-lap, 250-mile stock car race on a 3.2-mile course with 1.5-mile straightaways on the beach and on the asphalt road that ran parallel to the water. The sharp turns were on the loose sand.

Finding a sponsor, France joined the 1936 AAA Stock Car Race at Daytona Beach, which proved a grueling contest of endurance for the 27 drivers and cars that started. France and the other drivers faced heavily ploughed climbs, rough beach straightaways, and hazardous road twists. More than half of the entrants left due to smashups and mechanical failures, and

Top: A story appearing in the August 1937 issue of *Ford News* told how a specially built Matford equipped with an 85-horsepower V-8 engine and driven by a team of four women set 25 new world and international time and distance records in a 10-day continuous run at the Montlhéry Autodrome near Paris. **Center:** Ford dominated the 1938 Monte Carlo Rally, Europe's premier automotive race, when five Ford stock cars finished in the first seven places. **Bottom:** *Ford News* reported on the 1938 Gran Premio Nacional, where 15 of the 22 finishing cars were Fords. *All The Henry Ford*

In 1936, Daytona Beach held an 80-lap, 250-mile stock car race that ran on a 3.2-mile course comprising a mile and a half of straightaways on the beach and the asphalt road that ran parallel to the water. Sharp turns were located on the loose sand. Sponsored by American Automobile Association, the race began with 27 cars, including Ford V-8s, Lincoln-Zephyrs, Auburns, and Willys. Drivers faced heavily ploughed climbs, a rough beach straightaway, and hazardous road twists. More than half of the entrants left due to smashups and mechanical failures. Remarkably, Ford V-8s took all four prize-money places and 9 of the top 10 cars were V-8s, including that driven by Bill France Sr., who came in fifth place and would go on to found NASCAR. *The Henry Ford*

much success, but in 1938 a restaurant and nightclub owner named Charlie Reese took over and brought in France as a partner. They paid a $600 purse and split $200 in profits. The next year, France raised the ticket price from 50 cents to a dollar, netting $2,000.

As he learned the ropes of race promoting, France continued to race, working at his Daytona gas station at the corner of Halifax and Main during the week and driving on the weekends in many "outlaw" races (so named because the contests weren't sanctioned by AAA). During this time France met the likes of mechanic Red Vogt, Raymond Parks, and cousins Lloyd Seay and Roy Hall.

Bootlegger's Turn

When Prohibition started in 1920, moonshining became a thriving business in economically depressed regions of the Appalachians. Bootleggers used hopped-up cars to deliver illegal spirits to the thirsty populaces in cities such as Atlanta, Charlotte, Knoxville, and Winston-Salem.

Prohibition ended in 1933, but bootlegging didn't. Many Deep South counties remained dry—no alcoholic beverages of any kind could be made or sold. Where liquor was permitted, the U.S. government levied a tax. Many in the South scoffed at sending money to the North. The result was elaborate cat-and-mouse chases in the backwoods between bootleggers and the police and IRS federal agents or "revenuers." Success was determined by who had the fastest, most maneuverable car and the best driving skills.

practically every car was pulled out of the sand by a wrecking crew at some point. When the tide came in before the race was completed, Milt Marion of New York, who finished 75 laps, was declared the winner.

Remarkably Ford V-8s took all four prize-money places and 9 of the top 10 finishing cars were V-8s, including France's in fifth place.

An estimated 20,000 to 30,000 fans watched the 1936 race, but many had sneaked by the gates so the city lost thousands of dollars on the event, and the American Automobile Association withdrew. The 1937 race was run by the Elks Club, again without

Bootleggers stripped the interiors of their cars down to the driver's seat and added heavy springs in the rear to support a few hundred half-gallon Mason jars of moonshine. Of course, engines and transmissions were souped-up too.

When Ford's Atlanta assembly plant began churning out V-8s, they became the bootlegger's favorite car. One such daredevil was Lloyd Seay, a young man from Dawsonville, Georgia, located 60 miles north of Atlanta in the Blue Ridge Mountain region. In one story from his short bootlegging career, Seay was stopped for speeding through Roswell on his way back from making a delivery in Atlanta and handed over two $10 bills.

"Dammit, son, you ought to know by now the fine ain't but 10 dollars," the sheriff said.

"Hell, I know that, but I'm gon' be in a hurry comin' back, so I'm payin' in advance," Seay answered.

Seay's cousin Roy Hall, another bootlegger, was known to hold down the accelerator and never touch the brake pedal. In turns, when the car began to slip, he would accelerate, moving forward and sideways at the same time, turning the wheel in the same direction as the rear end if it began sliding too far one way.

Seay, Hall, and other drivers also developed a hair-raising 180-degree spin called the "bootlegger's turn" in order to flee from roadblocks. This involved hitting the brakes, tugging the emergency brake, and spinning the wheel. Many drove with their hands on the lower half of the steering wheel rather than at the upper half, so they could get more leverage.

Early Stock Car Racing

The two cousins teamed with a third cousin, Raymond Parks, an expatriate from Dawsonville. Parks had moved to Atlanta to be an entrepreneur and was a middleman in the moonshine business. He knew who made the whiskey and who wanted it. Master mechanic Vogt kept his cars running.

Like Bill France, Louis Jerome "Red" Vogt was born in Washington, D.C., and also raced, though he preferred motorcycles. In 1927, Vogt moved to Atlanta. Eventually, his skills at hopping up engines, especially Ford V-8s, earned

This picture taken in 1936 from the Southern Railway viaduct shows Ford's Atlanta branch assembly plant on Ponce de Leon Street. The plant, serving some 200 dealers in the Southeast, was built in 1913 and replaced after World War II. Given it's location and years of operation, it's certainly conceivable that the plant was the source of many a bootlegger's fast getaway car. *The Henry Ford*

139

THE WINNERS

1940 GILMORE-YOSEMITE ECONOMY RUN

Under Supervision of the A. A. A. Contest Board

W. R. Knapp (right), driver of the Mercury 8, smiles as he receives the championship trophy.

H. M. Jones (right), driver of the Lincoln-Zephyr, proudly displays the winner's trophy.

MERCURY 8
Winner in its class

23.76
MILES PER GALLON

LINCOLN-ZEPHYR V-12
Winner in its class

19.9
MILES PER GALLON

The Mercury 8, flashing up the steep, winding climb over lofty Chinquapin Pass. The route of the test run began near sea level and reached an altitude of more than 6,000 feet. Each driver was required to carry four passengers.

The Lincoln-Zephyr gets the winner's flag from an American Automobile Association director. Much of this grueling 300.5-mile run was made through dust and rain storms. The Lincoln-Zephyr was equipped with a two-speed overdrive axle.

In this same test run, the 85 hp Ford V-8 averaged 24.92 miles per gallon

Lloyd Seay, left, poses with car owner Raymond Parks after winning the 160-mile modified Daytona Beach Race on August 24, 1941. Driving a 1939 Ford, Seay led the entire 50 laps, defeating runner-up Joe Littlejohn by 31.2 miles. *Getty Images/ISC Archives*

Above: The class winners of the 1940 Gilmore-Yosemite Economy Run were a Mercury Eight and a Lincoln-Zephyr. Sponsored by the California-based Gilmore Oil Company and officiated by the American Automobile Association, these annual events were designed to show how fuel efficient cars were on a 314 1/2-mile-long mountain road from Los Angeles to Yosemite National Park. The 1940 Ford V-8-85 averaged 24.92 miles per gallon. A Ford V-8 also set a record in 1938 with a mark of 28.85 actual miles per gallon and a record of 50.767 miles per gallon on one section. The next most economical car in its class made 6.857 fewer miles per gallon. *The Henry Ford*

Right: Stock car racing was gaining in popularity just as World War II shut down nearly all forms of racing. Here at the 1940 Daytona Beach race, Bill France Sr. leads the pack around the north turn. France ran fourth in the March race and won the July event. *Getty Images/ISC Archives*

Fonty Flock captured the 1947 National Championship Stock Car Circuit championship and was also the 1949 NASCAR Modified champion. Above, he leads his brother Bob around the dirt track at Martinsville, Virginia, in 1948. *Both Getty Images/ISC Archives*

him and his Hemphill Service Station a favorable reputation with bootleggers.

After attending events at Lakewood, the local dirt track near Atlanta, Parks purchased new 1939 Ford coupes direct from Ford's Atlanta plant in 1939. With Seay and Hall's names painted on the sides along with "Hemphill Service Station," Parks entered the two in weekend races.

Both Hall and Seay won a number of races, including at Daytona. Seay won the 100-mile Labor Day race in 1941 at Lakewood against France, Hall, and drivers such as Bob Flock before a crowd of 15,000 people, taking home the $450 winner's purse. Despite a promising career as a race driver, Seay was murdered the next day (September 2) by a man who thought he had cheated him out of $120 on a transaction to purchase moonshine ingredients.

Seay's death impacted Parks but also Bill France, who later vowed to show drivers that racing was more profitable than moonshining. Like all other racing events, World War II stopped Southern stock car racing as France, Parks, and others were drawn into the fighting.

Oval-Track Dreams

As gas rationing disappeared after the war, servicemen returning home pulled junkers out of barns, yards, and scrap heaps. The weekend warriors used them on dirt tracks around the country. The California Roadster Association (CRA) started low-budget circle-track races around the state, while in the Midwest and along the East Coast stock car racing took hold. Still others used jalopies for demolition derbies, spelling the final end for many a late-1920s and 1930s car.

After working at Daytona Boat Works building sub-chasers during the war, Bill France returned to racing as a driver and promoter in 1946. Renting a dirt track at Charlotte, North Carolina, for what he promoted as a 100-mile championship race, he learned that to attract press coverage, he needed to develop a point system. He approached AAA for support, but was turned down.

AAA created its own stock car series, while France started the National Championship Stock Car Circuit. AAA declared France's organization and its races to be "outlaw," and a bitter rivalry between the groups developed.

The next big turn for stock car racing came at the July 4, 1946, race that France promoted at Greenville, South Carolina. Thousands of fans came out. Taking in $3,600 in profits, France later said the event "was the start of NASCAR" because it showed him racing was a moneymaker.

Raymond Parks returned as a veteran and survivor of the Battle of the Bulge, Nazi Germany's last great offensive in 1944 to break the Allied lines in Western Europe. Parks tapped the driving skills of several men, including Roy Hall; Gober Sosebee; Robert "Red" Byron, who had grown up in Colorado and dabbled in open-wheel racing; and the Flock brothers, Fonty and Bob, who partook in racing as well as bootlegging around Atlanta. Arguably, Parks became stock car racing's first multiple-car owner as he fielded 1939 Fords with engines tweaked by Red Vogt.

Growing up on a Dawsonville farm, Sosebee worked at Atlantic Steel during the Depression and started racing in late 1939 when he bought a new 1940 Ford from the assembly plant on Ponce de Leon Avenue in Atlanta. Soon after receiving the car in October 1939, he qualified in his first race and finished third. Because he was doing defense-related work at the steel mill, Sosebee avoided the draft. When he raced for Parks, he altered the interior of his '39 Ford with a contraption using truck springs and posts that attached to the roof of the car. Though some of the other drivers laughed at him, soon many were using similar roll bars to help prevent the roofs from crushing in during rollovers.

By the time of the 1947 Daytona race, arguments over what was stock and what wasn't grew worse. One driver had a 1934 Ford with a 1939 engine and a 1935 flywheel, so the car was disqualified. Another car was found to have red valve springs instead of standard green. The driver was thrown out. France recounted that that he only found out years later that "the color only identified where the spring was made and had nothing to do with its strength."

To resolve squabbles and create a more coherent sport, France called together 35 of the top mechanics, drivers, sponsors, and race promoters at the Streamline Hotel in Daytona Beach in December 1947. Many of the participants were stubborn, independent men, descendents of Confederates who had protested other men's laws. Yet out of the three-day meeting came the National Association for Stock Car Auto Racing with Bill France as president. NASCAR only allowed stock cars that were no more than three years old. Prewar Fords were banned and owners such as Parks and mechanics like Vogt had a hard time adjusting to the new rules.

Dry Lakes, Hot Rods

In the late 1930s, Southern California was the epicenter for youths on a quest for speed. This was mainly because of several geographical quirks located within 100 miles of Los Angeles: the dry lakes. Amid climate change thousands of years ago, water that covered the region dried up, leaving behind flat lake beds of clay, sand, and a variety of minerals devoid of vegetation. The resulting surface was perfect for young men (and a few women) to find out how fast their cars could go with little chance of running into anything.

The largest and most popular of the dry lakes was Muroc. At 10 miles wide and 22 miles long, Muroc was taken over by the army in 1940 and closed to racers (it is now home to Edwards Air Force Base). No problem—racers just shifted to the Harper, Rosamond, and El Mirage dry lakes.

One fellow who grew up knowing the dry lakes hot rodding scene is Dick Guldstrand. Better known today as "Mr. Corvette," Guldstrand was born in Santa Monica. His father took him to the races in the late 1930s, boosting him up on his shoulders.

"By the time I was 10 years old, I was hooked," Guldstrand said when interviewed in 2009. "You can't imagine the euphoria and the excitement of being part of an activity that was so dynamic. Here you'd get together with a bunch of friends and cohorts and you'd caravan out to El Mirage or Rosamond or whatever, and there would be a whole group of you sleeping on the desert with campfires and sleeping bags. When the sun came up, the lake bed was in perfect shape. We'd set up the timing equipment and run for the record."

The quest for speed spawned an entire cottage industry of tuners and speed equipment makers and merchants, including Dave Burns, Joe Davies, Vic Edelbrock, Kenny Harman, Jack Henry, Stuart Hilborn, Eddie Meyer, Ak Miller, Wayne Morrison, Mal Ord, Chuck Potvin, Tom Thickstun, Phil Weiand, Ed Winfield, Alex Xydias, and many others. These small businesses spawned the Speed (later renamed Specialty) Equipment Manufacturers Association, or SEMA.

Initially, most of the cars running at the lakes were older models—stripped-down Model T and A roadsters, with the

occasional Chevy or others equipped with four-banger engines. The windshields and often the fenders were removed to reduce wind resistance. Some racers began installing larger tires in the back (and smaller ones in front) for more traction on the lake, giving the roadsters a raked look. Some cars used Frontenac speed equipment developed for the inline fours.

When the Ford flathead V-8 became available, factory equipment was replaced with speed equipment such as Offenhauser or Navarro heads, Stromberg 97 or Winfield carburetors, overhead valves designed by Zora Arkus-Duntov, Howard or Iskenderian camshafts, Kong ignitions, and many others. Dual carburetors and milled heads were designed to increase the fuel-air mixture and compression ratio, respectively, and, hence, horsepower. Cylinders were bored larger to accommodate larger pistons with displacements going from 221 to 239 or 248 cubic inches. The 1938 Mercury V-8 engines allowed cylinders to be bored out to 268 cubic inches. By 1939, it was possible to get 130 horsepower from a V-8-85 engine. With an Ardun overhead-valve conversion kit, the Mercury V-8 engines achieved more than 300 horsepower.

The Southern California Timing Association (SCTA), formed in 1937—followed by the Western and the Russetta timing associations—organized competitions on the dry lakes and kept records. As street racing became a problem, the Los Angeles police chief derided the "100 mile per hour clubs" and threatened to take the "wild men" off the streets. The timing

associations made agreements with the police to ban from competition hot rodders who had been convicted of drunken driving, speeding, reckless driving, or street racing. After the attack on Pearl Harbor, however, only three meets were held on the lakes in 1942. Official racing was banned and, with gasoline rationed until the end of the war, however, only secret races were conducted until peacetime in 1945.

Golden Age of Hot Rodding

Many a dream was put on hold during the war. Some of those dreamers died on the battlefields of Europe, North Africa, the Pacific Islands, or in the cold seas between. When peace came, California became a hotbed of automotive racing, tuning, and customizing, populated by young men with newly acquired mechanical skills learned on Uncle Sam's dime.

Below: After World War II, returning servicemen pulled junkers out of barns, yards, and scrap heaps. These discarded automobiles became the raw materials for hot rods, stock cars, and demolition derbies. *The Henry Ford* **Right:** "Big Bill" Edwards, a long-time employee of Bell Auto Parts, drove his Cadillac-powered '40 Ford Standard Coupe every day on the street. With a GMC supercharger and four carburetors bolted to its 331-cubic-inch Cadillac mill, the car turned an incredible 150.12 miles per hour at the 1952 Bonneville Speed Trials and later appeared on the June 1953 cover of *Hot Rod Magazine*. *NHRA Museum*

HOT ROD

The Automotive "HOW-TO-DO-IT" Magazine

150 Mile Per Hour Street Coupe!
Page 40

JUNE 1953 25c

DUAL EXHAUST SYSTEMS
WHAT CAN THEY DO FOR '53 CARS?

Building a Hot Rod Sports Car

"Young men were getting out of the army, the air force, and so on. All this talent and technology came together and the hot rod movement exploded," Guldstrand said. "Edelbrock, 'Isky' Iskendarian, and all of the wonderful people who came out of the service with mechanical backgrounds and knowledge and started to play with cars. . . . When the auto people in Detroit realized what we were doing with the cars, they started showing up at our events."

The late 1940s and 1950s were the golden age of hot rods when the term came into widespread use to describe hopped-up, stripped-down cars. The SCTA swelled from 5 member clubs to 25 clubs. People raced on the dry lakes or at dirt tracks—and on the streets too. In 1946, SCTA members included AAA champion Rex Mays; three-time Indy 500 champion Lou Meyer; Wally Parks who would found the National Hot Rod Association (NHRA) in 1951; and Robert E. Petersen, who would found a publishing empire with *Hot Rod* magazine in 1948.

It was also the time when the 1937 to 1940 Fords became popular as hot rods. They were far newer than the early 1930s cars, modern looking, and had more up-to-date equipment. Roadsters, coupes, and the occasional two-door sedan made the cut for hot rodders. Four-door sedans were spurned because they were too much like a family car, while many hot rodders objected to the 1937 Fords altogether. Roadsters were the preferred hot rod style, since they were sporty and racy, but not enough of them had been made to go around.

The original V-8s were souped up and tires and gears were changed as the coupes took on a more raked look. And on the street, coupes and sedans had a significant advantage over roadsters: They blended in. When police went prowling for the "wild men," they might pass by the ordinary-looking hardtop—which might be a "sleeper" with a hopped-up mill under the hood.

Initially, the SCTA banned coupes and sedans from participating in timed events, but as street racing became

This golden 1940 De Luxe Coupe equipped with a tow bar was owned by Dick Miner of the prominent San Diego Prowlers Car Club. Built for both show and go, it was powered by a four-carb-equipped 331-cubic-inch Chrysler Hemi, and in 1960 was good for 110 miles per hour in the quarter-mile. *NHRA Museum*

A couple of street-driven hot rods—including a light-colored 1940 Ford De Luxe Coupe—face off in the Gas Coupe category at San Fernando Drag Strip in the late 1950s. Both are very typical Southern California street rods. *NHRA Museum*

dominated by those models, the Russetta Timing Association created a classification for coupes in 1948. Soon coupes—most of them Fords, of course—were posting speeds that exceeded many of the roadsters.

By the 1950s, the lakes racing scene began to fragment. Some enthusiasts began raising families, and their hot rods no longer fit their lifestyles. Others discovered the thrill of drag racing.

Dragsters

After 20 years of racing, many of the dry lakes had heavily rutted and dangerous surfaces. The best of the lakes, Muroc, was off limits. The Bonneville Salt Flats in the Great Salt Lake Desert was available—it's where the first Speed Week was held in

1949—but it was some 700 miles from Los Angeles. Meanwhile, police and city leaders continued to crack down on street races. Part of the thrill of hot rodding was just seeing how fast a car could jump off the line from a stop.

Santa Barbara Airport in Goleta, California, hosted the first legal drag racing event in 1948. From there, other impromptu races followed. Eighth- and quarter-mile drag strips opened across the country. It is believed nitromethane was first used for drag racing in a 1949 race at Santa Barbara in a Ford V-8 that had been bored out to 296 cubic inches. A year later, Edelbrock introduced its first nitro kits.

A majority of the early dragsters were stripped-down Fords because they had a good power-to-weight ratio, though the time

A 1937 Ford Coupe faces off with Jack Chrisman's famed Chrysler-powered '29 sedan at Pomona Raceway in 1954. NHRA rules from 1953 to 1955 and required fuel coupes and sedans to be stock-bodied and full-fendered. *NHRA Museum*

of the Ford/Mercury flathead V-8 was drawing to a close. In 1947, about 97 percent of the cars running in SCTA meets were powered by Ford engines, but then Chrysler's hemispherical V-8 came out in 1951. The final blow to the flathead came when Chevrolet debuted its lightweight, high-revving V-8 in late 1954. The Ford engines became a nostalgia item and were often swapped out of hot rods for newer powerplants.

Different car classes were developed and, oddly enough, even the 1937 "ugly duckling" Fords became the favorite of the Heavy Coupe class because they were the lightest.

"When I was growing up, I lusted after the '39 through '40 Fords," said Dave McClelland, veteran announcer of the NHRA when interviewed in 2009. "But my first race car was a '39 Chevy coupe with a fuel-injected 364 Buick and a LaSalle three-speed transmission. At the time, I thought it was the fastest car in the world."

By the time McClelland started announcing drag races in 1959, many of the cars were old, and the occasional '40 Ford would show up. New cars were limited to the Stock and Super Stock classes.

"I later owned a '40 Ford coupe with an LT1 Chevy, a turbo 400," McClelland added. "I drove it for a number of

Bob Goodman and Steve Sandirk had a great start to 1959. After winning the Competition Coupe/Sedan class at the Oakland Roadster Show, they took B/Fuel coupe class honors at the U.S. Fuel and Gas Championships in Bakersfield the first weekend in March, turning in the low 12-second range at 115 miles per hour with a 252-cubic-inch flathead. *NHRA Museum*

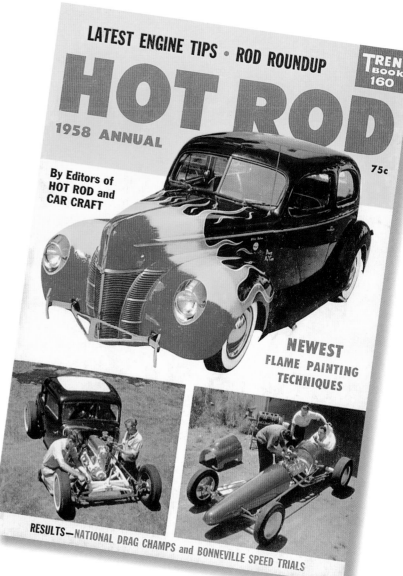

By the mid- and late 1950s, hot rod magazines were featuring '40 Fords on their covers, including Bob McCoy's iconic flamed Tudor Sedan (right). Though only in its teens, the '40 had already become a favorite of hot rodders. *Both John Sticha collection*

years and ended up trading it. . . . There is still a great deal of attraction of early cars because of their design. They're radically different from modern cars in appearance and with all the technological advances."

Rolling Sculptures

When the rich bought high-end cars such as Lincolns, Cords, Duesenbergs, and others, they weren't settling for the plain-Jane iron rolling out of Detroit's factories. They were ordering custom-bodied cars made to their desires. Traditional custom body shops died during the Depression, but the hot rodding culture kept the idea alive. While one part of hot rodding emphasized speed, the other stressed great looks and quality design.

Many of the sedan and coupe conversions after World War II were "show" rods with an emphasis on appearance rather than major engine work. Twin pipes might be added, chrome strips and door handles "shaved," bodies lowered, tops "chopped," wheel skirts and spotlights mounted, headlights and taillights "Frenched," and appointments such as bumpers, wheels, grilles, and hubcaps switched out for those of other makes that were deemed more aesthetically pleasing.

Hot rodding songs and album covers from artists like the Beach Boys, Jan and Dean, Dick Dale, the Ventures, and others, plus a spate of B-movies, mass-market paperbacks, and magazines featuring hot rods helped cement hot rodding and customizing into the fabric of American popular culture.

A number of custom designers who came upon the scene, including the Alexander Brothers, George and Sam Barris, Joe Bailon, Bill Cushenbery, Kenny "Von Dutch" Howard, Dean Jeffries, Ed "Big Daddy" Roth, Darryl Starbird, Harry Westergard, Joe Wilhelm, and others. Not surprisingly, the customizers and builders who gained the most notoriety in the hobby came out of California. One of the most prolific of these designers is Gene Winfield of Modesto, California. Involved in dry lakes and circle-track racing, he opened Winfield's Custom Shop in 1955 and went on to create many memorable cars, such as a 1956 Mercury called the *Jade Idol*.

Tom Hocker's 1940 De Luxe Coupe was customized by Tom, his brother, and Barris Kustoms in the mid-1950s. Updated in 1958 to incorporate quad headlights, it has a Cadillac engine and a top that's chopped 2 1/2 inches in front and 3 1/2 inches at the rear. The side grilles were filled and the fenders are molded to the body. *NHRA Museum*

Earle Bruce's 1940 De Luxe Coupe appeared on the cover of the February '52 issue of *Hot Rod Magazine* (left) as "California's Most Customized Coupe." Built by such customizing pioneers as Chuck Porter and Jimmy Summers, its top is chopped 3 3/4 inches and the quarter windows are filled. *NHRA Museum*

FEBRUARY 1952 25¢

WHAT TO DO ABOUT FENDERS?

HOT ROD
MAGAZINE

CALIFORNIA'S MOST CUSTOMIZED COUPE *See Page 16*

Photographer Dave Cunningham's 1940 Sedan achieved its low profile from a body that he sectioned and then channeled over the frame. The fenders had to be raised and the hood sectioned to compensate. Candy apple red paint was sprayed by Hal Hutchins. *NHRA Museum*

Interviewed in 2009, Winfield was working on a 1940 Mercury convertible, giving it a chopped top, fiberglass panels, and more. The 1940 Fords "are a good looking design," he noted. "My first metal-flake paint job was on a '40 Ford coupe. And, I didn't paint it just one color; I painted it in a rainbow of colors. . . . It was lacquered and with the old metal flake, you had to put on many coats of clear. It had to be sanded until you got it flat."

Today, the 1940 Ford is one of the best designs for street rodding, added Larry Erickson of Detroit's College for Creative Studies. "When hot rodding came back in the 1970s, these cars drew people because they have expressive curves. They have enough room to put in five adults, while the '32 Ford is good for two adults and three kids in the back."

To contemporary buyers, the 1937–1940 Fords captured and represented the streamlined, modern aerodynamic look that was very appealing to a public ready to take to the "Road

of Tomorrow." Today, their beautiful aesthetics continue to attract collectors and hot rodders. Bob Gregorie and Edsel Ford didn't follow General Motors' design cues but blazed their own path. The cars picked up on the optimism that prevailed as the Depression wound down and before the world went to war.

The 1937 to 1940 Fords were not made to be flashy or to be muscle cars like the later-day Chevrolet Corvette, Ford Mustang, Pontiac GTO, or Dodge Challenger. They were made to be fast and rugged, which explains their longevity with collectors.

Many of the cars' innovative design features, quirks, and flaws can be credited to the mechanical genius and stubbornness of Henry Ford and the persistence of his son, Edsel. The power plays that developed among Henry, Edsel, and Ford executives notwithstanding, they not only made cars that lasted the test of time, they built a company that keeps going.

Countless '40 Fords were smashed beyond repair on local dirt tracks or died slow, rusty deaths in cluttered junkyards. Not surprisingly, those cars that remain—many of them saved from dusty barns and lonely fields—are popular platforms among today's hot rodders and customizers.

Facing: At the time this convertible was photographed around 2000, it was owned by Monty and Tania Lewellen. It was running a 350 small-block Chevy with an M-21 Muncie four-speed transmission and a Ford 9-inch rearend. The chrome wheels and Cal Custom axle covers are perfect, and the seaweed-type flames nicely accentuate the distinctive Forty lines.

Clockwise from top left: This Sedan Delivery sat in a barn for 40 years before it was discovered by David Lyon. Today it's owned by Richie Whalen and is the official shop truck and Bonneville push car for the Rolling Bones hot rod shop out of upstate New York. The car also served as a Bonneville push car back in 1962 and still runs a flathead.

Jim Johnson is the third owner of this patinaed '40 De Luxe Coupe. He got the car in 1986 and it sat alongside his garage for 19 years (it had sat for 20 years before that). He took just four months to drop in a 350 Chevy topped with a brace of three two-barrel carburetors. The interior is original, just like that paint.

The Standard Coupe was photographed at Utah's Bonneville Salt Flats in 2008. The owner, Bob Basso, had driven it down from Bozeman Montana to attend Speedweek. The primered rear fender is as perfect as the stance.

Ric White's hoodless '40 runs a small-block Chevy motor with two four-barrel carburetors. The 15-inch tires mounted on chrome steelies nicely complement the flat black paint and flames. In this profile

Bibliography

Books

Arnold, Marvin. *Lincoln and Continental Classic Motorcars: The Early Years*. Dallas, TX: Taylor Publishing Co., 1989.

Babson, Steve, with Ron Alpern, Dave Elsila, and John Revitte. *Working Detroit*. Detroit: Wayne State University Press, 1986.

Banham, Russ. *The Ford Century: Ford Motor Company and the Innovations That Shaped the World*. San Diego, CA: Tehabi Books, 2002.

Barnard, John. *Walter Reuther and the Rise of the Auto Workers*. Boston: Little, Brown and Company, 1983.

Bennett, Harry Herbert, with Paul Marcus. *We Never Called Him Henry*. New York: Gold Medal, 1951.

Breer, Carl (edited by Anthony J. Yanik). *The Birth of Chrysler Corporation and Its Engineering Legacy*. Warrendale, PA: Society of Automotive Engineers, 1995.

Bootle, Benny, with Thomas E. Christenberry, Freddie Copeland, Marll McDonald, and Wayne Moore. *The 1940 Ford Book: A Compendium of Current Restoration Practices*. San Leandro, CA: The Early Ford V-8 Club of America, Inc., 1987.

Boyer, Richard O., and Herbert M. Morais. *Labor's Untold Story*. New York: United Electrical, Radio & Machine Workers of America, 1974.

Brierley, Brooks T. *Magic Motors 1930*. Coconut Grove, FL: Garrett and Stringer, Inc., 1996.

Brooke, Lindsay. *Ford Model T: The Car That Put the World on Wheels*. St. Paul, MN: Motorbooks, 2008.

Bryan, Ford. *Henry's Lieutenants*. Detroit: Wayne State University Press, 1993.

———. *Rouge: Pictured in Its Prime*. Detroit: Wayne State University Press, 2003.

Burgess-Wise, David. *Ford at Dagenham: The Rise and Fall of Detroit in Europe*. Derby, UK: Breedon Books Publishing Co., 2007.

Cabadas, Joseph P. *River Rouge: Ford's Industrial Colossus*. St. Paul, MN: MBI Publishing, 2004.

Cheetham, Craig, general editor. *American Cars: The Automobiles that Made America*. London: Amber Books, 2004.

Clark, Sally H. *Trust and Power: Consumers, the Modern Corporation, and the Making of the United States Automobile Market*. New York: Cambridge University Press, 2007.

Collier, Peter, and David Horowitz. *The Fords: An American Epic*. New York: Simon & Schuster, 1987.

Cray, Ed. *Chrome Colossus: General Motors and Its Times*. New York: McGraw-Hill Book Co., 1980.

Dahlinger, John Côté, with Frances Spatz Leighton. *The Secret Life of Henry Ford*. Indianapolis, IN: The Bobbs-Merrill Co., 1978.

Dominguez, Henry. *Edsel: The Story of Henry Ford's Forgotten Son*. Warrendale, PA: Society of Automotive Engineers, Inc., 2002.

Duffield, Edgar N. *Ford Through European Eyeglasses 1907–1947*. Chelmsford, UK: The Mercury Press Ltd., 1948.

Edsall, Larry. *Masters of Car Design*. Vercelli, Italy: Edizioni White Star Publishers S.r.l., February 2008.

Farrell, James, and Cheryl Farrell. *Ford Design Department Concepts and Show Cars: 1932–1961*. Hong Kong: World Print Ltd., 1999.

Faulkner, Harold U., and Mark Starr. *Labor in America*. New York: Oakford Book Co., 1955.

Fine, Sidney. *Sitdown: The General Motors Strike of 1936–1937*. Ann Arbor, MI: The University of Michigan Press, 1969.

Grant, David. *The Legendary Custom Cars and Hot Rods of Gene Winfield*. St. Paul, MN: Motorbooks, 2008.

Halberstam, David. *The Reckoning*. New York: Avon Books, 1986.

Hanks, David A., and Anne Hoy. *American Streamlined Design: The World of Tomorrow*. Paris: Editions Flammarion, 2005.

Hemphill, Paul. *Wheels: A Season on NASCAR's Winston Cup Circuit*. New York: Simon & Schuster, 1997.

Lacey, Robert. *Ford: The Men and the Machine*. New York: Little Brown and Company, 1986.

Lamm, Michael, and Dave Holls. *A Century of Automotive Style: 100 Years of American Car Design*. Stockton, CA: Lamm-Morada Publishing Co., 1996.

Langworth, Richard M., and Jan P. Norbye. *The Complete History of General Motors 1908–1986*. New York: Beekman House, 1986.

Lasky, Victor. *Never Complain, Never Explain: The Story of Henry Ford II*. New York: Richard Marek Publishers, 1981.

Lee, Albert. *Henry Ford and the Jews*. New York: Stein and Day, 1980.

Levin, Leo. *Ford: The Dust and the Glory, A Racing History, Vol. 1 (1901–1967)*. Warrendale, PA: Society of Automotive Engineers, Inc., 2000.

Lewis, Eugene W. *Motor Memories: A Saga of Whirling Gears*. Detroit: Alved, Publishers, 1947.

Mallast, Gary J. *The 1938–39 Ford Book: For Passenger Cars*. San Leandro, CA: The Early Ford V-8 Club of America, Inc., 2002.

Marcus, Sheldon. *Father Coughlin: The Tumultuous Life of the Priest of the Little Flower*. Boston: Little, Brown and Company, 1973.

Mays, James C. *Ford and Canada: 100 Years Together*. Montreal: Syam Publishing, 2003.

Montgomery, Don. *Hot Rods As They Were*. Los Angeles: Bradshaw Bros. Press, 1989.

Nevins, Allan, and Frank Ernest Hill. *Ford: Decline and Rebirth 1933–1962*. New York: Charles Scribner's Sons, 1963.

———. *Ford: Expansion and Challenge 1915–1932*. New York: Charles Scribner's Sons, 1957.

Olsen, Byron, and Dan Lyons. *Station Wagons*. St. Paul, MN: MBI Publishing, 2000.

Olsen, Byron, and Joseph P. Cabadas. *The American Auto Factory*. St. Paul, MN: MBI Publishing, 2002.

Peters, George, and Henri Greuter. *Novi: The Legendary Indianapolis Race Car: Vol. One: The Welch Years (1941–1960)*. Hazelwood, MO: Bar Jean Enterprises, 1991.

Post, Dan R. *Ford V8 Service Bulletins 1932–1937 Complete*. Arcadia, CA: Post Motor Books, 1968.

———. *Ford V8 Service Bulletins 1938–1940 Complete*. Arcadia, CA: Post Motor Books, 1970.

Reuther, Victor G. *The Brothers Reuther: And the Story of the UAW/A Memoir*. Boston: Houghton Mifflin Co., 1976.

Silk, Gerald. *Automobile and Culture*. New York: Harry N. Abrams, Inc., 1984.

Sorensen, Charles E. *My Forty Years with Ford*. New York: W. W. Norton & Co., 1956.

Sorensen, Lorin. *The Classy Ford V8*. St. Helena, CA: Silverado Publishing Co., 1982.

Thacker, Tony. *'32 Ford Deuce: The official 75th anniversary edition*. St. Paul, MN: Motorbooks, 2007.

Thompson, Neal. *Driving with the Devil: Southern Moonshine, Detroit Wheels, and the Birth of NASCAR*. New York: Three Rivers Press, 2006.

Tzouliadis, Tim. *The Forsaken: An American Tragedy in Stalin's Russia*. New York: The Penguin Press, 2008.

Upward, Geoffrey C. *A Home for Our Heritage: The Building and Growth of Greenfield Village and Henry Ford Museum, 1929–1979*. Dearborn, MI.: Henry Ford Museum Press, 1979.

Werling, Donn P. *Henry Ford: A Hearthside Perspective*. Warrendale, PA: Society of Automotive Engineers, Inc., 2000.

Woudenberg, Paul R. *Ford in the Thirties*. Los Angeles: Petersen Publishing Co., 1976.

Wrynn, V. Dennis. *Detroit Goes to War: The American Automobile Industry in World War II*. Osceola, WI: Motorbooks, 1993.

Periodicals

"1st Quarter Output Is Set at 1,270,000: Represents Gain of 13 Per Cent Over Similar 1936 Period." *Automobile Topics* (April 5, 1937).

"2 Motor Magnates Back from Europe: Sloan, Edsel Ford, Return, Talk of Conditions." *Automobile Topics* (September 5, 1938).

"75 Candles." *Ford News* (August 1938).

"1940 Ford, Lincoln-Zephyr, Mercury." *Ford News* (October 1940).

"1940 Ford V-8 Trucks and Commercial Vehicles." *Ford News* (October 1939).

"1940 Introductions Coast to Coast: Ford V-8, Mercury 8, Lincoln-Zephyr V-12." *Ford News* (November 1939).

"A Bigger, Better Ford Ten: Attractive New Model from Dagenham." *The Irish Motor News* (April 22, 1937).

"About 25,500,000 Cars Are Now on Roads: Last Year's Registrations Showed 3,480,253 New." *Automobile Topics* (June 6, 1938).

"Accessories Sold as Christmas Presents: Chevrolet Merchandising Mgr. Reports Widespread Buying." *Automobile Topics* (December 16, 1935).

"A Day With Ford: Dealers of Canada and United States in First Convention." *Ford News* (December 1936).

"A Forest Village." *Ford News* (October 1937).

"A New Farm Market." *Ford News* (September 1938).

"A New Ford V-8: Attractive 22 hp Model for Free State Market." *The Irish Motor News* (December 17, 1936).

"Another Village Industry." *Ford News* (March 1937).

"At Daytona Beach." *Ford News* (May 1, 1936).

"At the Shows" and ""The World Greets the 1937 Ford V-8." *Ford News* (December 1936).

"At Ypsilanti." *Ford News* (April 1937).

"Author Who Was Russian Prisoner Dies; American Victor Herman Held 18 Years; Ordeal Became TV Film." *Los Angeles Times* (March 29, 1985).

"Automobile Labor Front Embroiled in CIO Fight: UAW Split Wide Open." *Automobile Topics* (June 27, 1938).

"Automotive Influence Strong in New Zephyr-type Train." *Automobile Topics* (October 14, 1935).

"Automobile Labor Front Embroiled in CIO Fight: UAW Split Wide Open." *Automobile Topics* (June 27, 1938).

"Automobile Output on Upward Swing: Capacity Operations Predicted within Next Few Weeks." *Automobile Topics* (April 19, 1937).

"Average Car Found to be 4.71 Yrs. Old: Average Life Set at 8.40 Yrs., Against 7.04 Yrs. In 1926." *Automobile Topics* (Nov. 16, 1936).

"A Visit to Dagenham." *The Irish Motor News* (July 7, 1932).

Bonin, Hubert. "Ford and the Second World War in Continental Europe." *Ford, 1903–2003: The European History Volume I*. Paris: Editions P.L.A.G.E., 2003.

———. "The Ford Brand's Image, It's Evolution in Europe from the 1930s to the 1980s." *Ford, 1903–2003: The European History Volume I*. Paris: Editions P.L.A.G.E., 2003.

———. "The Rise of Ford in Britain: From Sales Agency to Market Leader, 1904–1980." *Ford: The European History, Vol. II*. Paris: Editions P.L.A.G.E., 2003.

"Briefly Told." *Ford News* (September 1939).

"British Car Taxes Raised Very Sharply: Fear Effect upon American Designs under New Levy." *Automobile Topics* (May 1, 1939).

"British Ford Shows Increase in Output: £100 Popular Ford Volume Was Doubled During 1936." *Automobile Topics* (June 7, 1936).

"British Manufacturer Here." *Automobile Topics* (Nov. 2, 1936).

"Brooklyn Another Village Industry." *Ford News* (December 1939).

Calkins, Earnest Elmo. "Beauty the New Business Tool." *Atlanta Monthly* (CXL, August 1927).

Cantor, George. "Detroit's Killer Heat Wave of 1936." *The Detroit News* (August 4, 1996).

"Dealers at Dearborn: Gather to View New 1937 Line and to Present Gift to Village." *Ford News* (November 1936).

Donnelly, Jim. "Novi Governor Special." *Hemmings Muscle Machines* (October 1, 2004).

Emanuel, Dave. "Henry Ford's Wild Irishman." *Super Ford* (February 1989).

"Employment Is Near Peak." *Automobile Topics* (May 3, 1937).

"Epidemic of Strikes Is Slowly Spreading: Industrial Indices Not Affected Yet But Trouble Zone Widens." *Automobile Topics* (January 11, 1937).

Epstein, Alex. "Government Spending Didn't End the Great Depression." *Atlantic Sentinel* (April 22, 2010).

"Europe's Greatest Race." *Ford News* (April 1938).

"Eyes of the Nation on Used Car Week: Epoch-Making Sales Campaign Underway." *Automobile Topics* (March 7, 1938).

"Ford 1939 Mercury." *Automobile Topics* (November 7, 1938).

"Ford 1940 Program Calls for 900,000 Units." *Automobile Topics* (October 9, 1939).

"Ford and Lewis Typify Conflict of Ideas in Business Philosophy." *Automobile Topics* (November 1, 1937).

"Ford at the 1940 Fairs." *Ford News* (April 1940).

"Ford Bantam Models Disclose Refinements." *Automobile Topics* (February 13, 1932).

"Ford Begins Operations at Vancouver Plant." *Automobile Topics* (July 25, 1938).

"Ford Calls First Factory Meeting: 7,000 Dealers to Visit Dearborn, Mich., Plant on Nov. 6." *Automobile Topics* (November 2, 1936).

"Ford Co. to Aid British Workers Called to War: Pay Continued for 3 Months." *Automobile Topics* (November 20, 1939).

"Ford Gains in Fight Against NLRB Rule." *Automobile Topics* (May 16, 1938).

"Ford Holds First Factory Meeting: 8,000 Dealers Attend Dearborn Party As Guests of Company." *Automobile Topics* (November 9, 1936).

"Ford Introducing 'COE' Truck Models: New Units Arranged to Be Easily Serviced." *Automobile Topics* (May 23, 1938).

"Ford Is Honored on His 75th Birthday: Detroit and Dearborn Pay Him Deserved Tribute." *Automobile Topics* (August 1, 1938).

"Ford Is Planning to Blanket the Field: The Outlook Influenced by Unannounced Project." *Automobile Topics* (November 15, 1937).

"Ford Line Includes New 60 HP. Engine: Two Engine Sizes Available in The Single Chassis." *Automobile Topics* (November 16, 1936).

"Ford Line Includes Two Engine Sizes: 60 and 85 Horsepower Models Offers on 112-In. Wheelbase." *Automobile Topics* (November 9, 1936).

"Ford Making Trucks of Two-Speed Axles: May Be Obtained in School Bus Chassis Also." *Automobile Topics* (April 25, 1938).

"Ford Marketing Developments." *The Irish Motor News* (June 16, 1932).

"Ford Moves Forward with a Broader 1938 Line and $40,000,000 Plant Expansion Program." Ford advertisement. *Automobile Topics* (October 25, 1937).

"Ford New Zealand." *Ford News* (October 1937).

"Ford on Treasure Island." *Ford News* (February 1939).

"Ford Pageant Brings Back Yesterdays . . . Foretells Future." *Radco Automotive Review* (November 1933).

"Ford Predicts 1939 Sales Rise of 50%: Output of Ford Plants to Total 750,000." *Automobile Topics* (October 31, 1938).

"Ford Revises Prices; Delivery Basis Cut: To Show 1940 Models at Hotel Astor." *Automobile Topics* (October 9, 1939).

"Ford Says His Workers May 'Join Anything.'" *Automobile Topics* (April 19, 1937).

"Ford Sets '37 Goal of 1,300,000 Cars." *Automobile Topics* (November 16, 1936).

"Ford Starts Up New Tire-Making Plant: Is Building Own Tires on Special Type Machinery." *Automobile Topics* (June 6, 1938).

"Ford Swinging into Production." *Automobile Topics* (November 9, 1936).

"Ford Truck Offers Smart New Lines: Choice of Power to Fit Individual Requirements Provided." *Automobile Topics* (November 16, 1936).

"Ford Trucks: Three Engines, Wide Choice of Equipment." *Automobile Topics* (October 31, 1938).

"Gains by Diesels, More Models, New Trucks, Outlook." *Automobile Topics* (November 7, 1938).

"General Motors II: Chevrolet." *Fortune* (January 1939).

"German Cars Flood England." *Automobile Topics* (May 23, 1938).

"Good-Bye to All That: The I.M.R.C. Races in Phoenix Park." *The Irish Motor News* (September 21, 1939).

"Government Spending Didn't End the Great Depression." *Atlantic Sentinel* (April 22, 2010).

"Green Island: Where Four Friends Camped, Ford Plant Now Makes Parts." *Ford News* (August 1937).

"Handy Conditioner Delays Oil Change: 'Percolite,' New Purifying Element, Increases Life of Lubricant." *Automobile Topics* (April 20, 1936).

"Henry Ford and the Ferguson Tractor." *The Irish Motor News* (May 18, 1939).

"Home Brew: Some Interesting Irish Built Racing Cars." *The Irish Motor News* (August 10, 1939).

"Improvement Noted in New Car Market: Used Car Sales Are Not Sharing the Upswing." *Automobile Topics* (November 15, 1937).

"Industry in the Country." *Ford News* (April 1938).

Kibira, Deogratias, and Charles R. McLean. *Generic Simulation of Automotive Assembly for Interoperability Testing.* Maryland: Manufacturing Systems Integration Division, National Institute of Standards and Technology, 2007.

"Labor Act Upheld by Supreme Court: Way Is Cleared for Rigorous Enforcement of Wagner Law." *Automobile Topics* (April 19, 1937).

"Labor Embraces 'The Revolution.'" *Automobile Topics* (April 27, 1936).

"Labor Pushes Drive on Motor Industry." *Automobile Topics* (January 4, 1937).

Lamm, Michael. "Gilded Fords: The flathead V-8 and the cautious rich kept custom builders alive during the Depression." *Car Life* (February 1970).

Lewis, David L. "Harry Bennett, Ford's Tough Guy: Part 1." *Cars & Parts* (circa mid-1980s). Originally published in the *Detroit Free Press* (circa 1973).

"Lewis Pounds Away at General Motors: But Strike Leadership Is Periled by Anti-Union Movement." *Automobile Topics* (January 11, 1937).

"Lincoln-Zephyr Adds Four New Body Styles in 1938 Line Which Features Longer Wheelbases and Improvements of Design." *Automobile Topics* (October 25, 1937).

"Lincoln-Zephyr Bold Innovation." *Automobile Topics* (November 4, 1936).

"Little Plants in the Country." *Ford News* (July 1936).

"Looking at 1935 in Perspective." *Automobile Topics* (December 30, 1935).

Loubet, Jean-Louis, and Nicolas Hatzfeld. "Ford in France, 1916–1955: From an American dream to a failure," from Hubert Bonin and eds. *Ford, 1903–2003: The European History, Volume II.* Paris: Editions P.L.A.G.E., 2003.

Ludvigsen, Karl. "John Tjaarda: One Man's Quest for the Ideal Car." *Automobile* (January 1968).

"Lunch Rooms and Showers." *Ford News* (March 1939).

"Martin Holds Ford Will Sign During 1939: UAW Head Predicts Contractual Agreement with Company." *Automobile Topics* (August 29, 1938).

"Milford Another Village Industry." *Ford News* (September 1939).

"Mr. Ford Doesn't Care." *Fortune.* (VIII, December 1933).

"More Car Builders Adopt Conditioning: Experiments Carried on By Several Makers." *Automobile Topics* (February 21, 1938).

"More New Ford Models: Alternative Engines Available in New V-8." *The Irish Motor News.* (January 14, 1937).

"More War Talk in U.S. Than Abroad." *Automobile Topics* (June 28, 1937).

"Motor Briefs: News of Interest to Michigan Automobile Owners." *Motor News* (May 1940).

"Motor Industry Converges on 1938." *Automobile Topics* (October 25, 1937).

"Motoring in Germany: Enlightened Views on Value of Sport to the State." *The Irish Motor News* (June 4, 1936).

"National Used Car Week March 5 to 12: Macauley Reveals Plan to Break the Jam." *Automobile Topics* (February 28, 1938).

"New Car Domestic Sales by Makes." *Automotive Industries* (February 22, 1930).

"New Cars Moving in Early March Survey." *Automobile Topics* (March 14, 1938).

"New Car Production Recovers Strength: Ford, Willys Resume on 1938s; Late Season Sales Good." *Automobile Topics* (August 22, 1938).

"New Fords Described as Production for '38 Starts." *Automobile Topics* (November 29, 1937).

"New Plant Opened at Northville." *Ford News* (February 1937).

"New Models Brighter in Color, Survey Shows: Black Drops into Fourth Place." *Automobile Topics* (December 7, 1936).

"New York Is Shown Ford's 1938 Models: Price Increase Is Less Than Was Anticipated." *Automobile Topics* (November 1, 1937).

Noble, William T. "The Chrysler Airflow: Flop in 1930s Is Big Hit Today." *The Detroit News* (December 20, 1964).

"No European Depression, Ford Official Asserts: General Manager Back." *Automobile Topics* (May 16, 1938).

"Odds and Ends." *The Irish Motor News* (April 20, 1939).

Oliver, John. "Situation in England: Improvements Made in Economy, Riding Qualities, Performance—Body Styles Still Conservative." *Automobile Topics* (December 5, 1938).

"One Foot in the Soil, One Foot in Industry." *Ford News* (April 1937).

"Only Ford Turning Out 1936 Models: Two Announcements Scheduled for Middle of September." *Automobile Topics* (September 7, 1936).

Pace, Eric. "Prince Louis Ferdinand, 86, Grandson of Kaiser, Is Dead." *The New York Times* (September 27, 1994).

"Pick-up Box for the Coupe." *Ford News* (April 1937).

"Plymouth Built 2,000,000 Cars in Eight Years: 1,000,000 Produced in 1934." *Automobile Topics* (December 7, 1936).

"Pre-Approved for Service." *Ford News* (October 1939).

"Progress in the Ford World 1938." *Ford News* (January 1939).

"Progress in the Ford World 1939." *Ford News* (January 1940).

Radco Automotive Review (November 1933).

"Rear-Engine Cars Are Here." *Motor* (December 1933).

"Rear Engine Cars Next?" *Automobile Topics* (March 28, 1931).

Ricker, Chester S. "Many Improvements in Spite of Appearances." *Automobile Topics* (November 1, 1937).

Ricker, Chester S. "What's New in the 1936 Cars?" *Automobile Topics* (November 11, 1935).

Roper, Daniel C. "The Automobile Industry— Its Achievements and Responsibilities." *Automobile Topics* (November 11, 1935).

"'Sealed Beam' Lights Ready for Industry." *Automobile Topics* (August 21, 1939).

"Sees American Sales Undaunted by Wars: Sherlock Holds Sales Will Be Maintained." *Automobile Topics* (October 3, 1938).

"Sees Used Car Jam Disguised Blessing: Veteran of Business Calls Situation a 'Strike.'" *Automobile Topics* (February. 28, 1938).

Seims, Charles. "Henry's Legacy: The Unconventional Story of the Ford V-8," magazine unknown, from the files of the National Automotive History Collection, Detroit Public Library.

Shlaes, Amity. "The Legacy of the 1936 Election." *Imprimis* (September 2007).

"'Sit-down' Strike Typifies new Trend in Trade Unionism." *Automobile Topics* (June 15, 1936).

"Springtime in Motordome." *Motor News* (April 1939).

"Soy Bean Factory Starts." *Automobile Topics* (August 22, 1938).

"Station Wagons Go Custom." *Automobile Topics* (March 25, 1940).

"Stiff Competition: Lower Medium Price Range, $775 to $925 Now Includes 10 Four Door Sedans, With 10 More at $50 Either Way." *Automobile Topics* (November 7, 1938).

"The 1939 Ford V-8 Trucks and Commercial Cars: Giving Economy a New Meaning over a Wider Range of Today's Haulage and Delivery Options." *Ford News* (November 1938).

"The 100,000th Mercury 8 Goes West." *Ford News* (February 1940).

"The 27,000,000th Car Returns to Treasure Island." *Ford News* (August 1939).

"The Ford 'Baby' Makes Its Debut." *The Irish Motor News* (February 25, 1932).

"The Ford Exhibition: One-make Show at the Albert Hall." *The Irish Motor News* (October 21, 1937).

"The Ford Motor Exhibition." *The Irish Motor News* (October 27, 1932).

"The Ford Show: Third Annual Exhibition in Dublin." *The Irish Motor News* (February 11, 1937).

"The Ford V-8." *Ford News* (October 1939).

"The Ford V-8 Station Wagons for 1939." *Ford News* (November 1938).

"The Gran Premio Nacional." *Ford News* (January 1939).

"The New Models." *Motor News* (November 1938).

"The Second Ford Exhibition: Comprehensive Display at the Mansion House." *The Irish Motor News* (February 13, 1936).

"The World Comes to Treasure Island." *Ford News* (March 1939).

"The World Greets the 1937 Ford V-8." *Ford News* (December 1936).

"The World of Tomorrow" and "The Road of Tomorrow." *Ford News* (April 1939).

Thomes, Paul. "Searching for Identity: Ford Motor Company in the German Market (1903–2003)." *Ford: The European History, Vol. II.* Paris: Editions P.L.A.G.E., 2003.

Tolliday, Steven. "The Origins of Ford of Europe: From Multidomestic to Transnational Corporation, 1903–1976," from Hubert Bonin and eds. *Ford, 1903–2003: The European History, Volume I.* Paris: Editions P.L.A.G.E., 2003.

———. "The Rise of Ford in Britain: From Sales Agency to Market Leader, 1904–1980," *Ford: The European History, Vol. II.* Paris: Editions P.L.A.G.E., 2003.

Trepagnier, William J., editor. "About the New Cars." *Motor News* (October 1939).

———. "Picking the Winners." *Motor News* (November 1938).

"Typical Families." *Ford News* (June 1940).

"Used Car Exchange Week Is Held Successful: Incomplete Returns Show a Substantial Volume." *Automobile Topics.* (March 14, 1938).

Wilkins, Mira. "Ford among Multinational Companies," from Hubert Bonin and eds. *Ford, 1903–2003: The European History, Volume I.* Paris: Editions P.L.A.G.E., 2003.

Vance, Bill. "Motoring Memories: William Stout and His Scarab." *Canadian Driver* (July 29, 2005).

"Village Industries by Little Rivers." *Ford News* (April 1936).

Web

Auto Editors of *Consumer Guide.* "1936 Stout Scarab." *HowStuffWorks.com*, http://auto. howstuffworks.com/1936-stout-scarab.htm (accessed October 23, 2007).

Guldstrand, Dick. www.theautochannel.com/ cybercast/carguy/1997/0610.html.

Johnson, Dale. "How the Big Three Survived Depression: GM, Chrysler Overtook Ford and Prospered, Reversing Today's Roles for the Detroit Makers." *Wheels.ca* www.wheels.ca/ article/545311 (accessed May 9, 2009).

Interviews

Alpern, Ron. Interviewed by author. March 15, 2001.

Casey, Robert H., John and Horace Dodge Curator of Transportation at The Henry Ford. Interviewed by author. Digital recording, March 27, 2009.

Cousins, Ross. Interviewed by author. Digital recording, May 3, 2010.

Crain, Keith E., chairman of Crain Communications, Inc. Interviewed by author. Digital recording, March 10, 2009.

Davis, Michael. Interviewed by author. Digital recording, January 31, 2010.

Erikson, Larry. Interviewed by author. Digital recording, December 1, 2009.

Guldstrand, Dick, owner Guldstrand Motorsports. Interviewed by author. Digital recording, February 20, 2009.

Ford, Steve. Interviewed by author. Various times, 2009.

Kreipke, Robert. Interviewed by author. February 15, 2010.

Kuhr, Tom. Interviewed by author. Dearborn, MI, January 20, 2010.

Maher, Charles, artist and former Ford Motor Company designer. Interviewed by author. E-mail, February 23, 2009.

McClelland, Dave, NHRA announcer. Interviewed by author. March 6, 2009.

Mook, Howard D. "Buck," retired Ford designer. Interviewed by author. February 2, 2009.

Moore, Derek, conservation specialist, The Henry Ford. Interviewed by author. Digital recording, March 27, 2009.

Schneider, Ron. Interviewed by author. Digital recording, May 12, 2010.

Smith, Larry. Interviewed by author. Digital recording, May 11, 2010.

Tjaarda, Tom. Interviewed by author. E-mail, March 5, 2010.

Watson, Ron, president of the Motorsports Hall of Fame of America. Interviewed by author. Digital recording, February 11, 2009.

Winfield, Gene. Interviewed by author. Digital recording, Detroit, March 6, 2009.

Speeches

Ford, Edsel Bryant II. "Keynote Speech About Legacy of Henry Ford and the Model T." Model T Club of America's Centennial T Party, Richmond, IN, July 2008.

Films

It's Ford for 1940. Lorin Sorensen Productions.

Letters, Memorandum, Forms, Pamphlets, Reminiscences, and Organizational Files

"22 Reasons Why Business Is Better—And Why Lincoln Sales Will Increase in 1936." Ford Motor Company brochure, October 1935.

"1941 Ford V-8 Fordor Sedan." Ford News Bureau, #74387-D, 1953.

"27,000,000th Ford Arrives at New York Fair." Ford News Bureau, June 16, 1939.

"AAA Head Attends Good Drivers League Contest." Ford News Bureau, 1940.

"Albert Kahn: The American Institute of Architects 2002 Gold Medal Submission." Albert Kahn Associates, Inc., 2001.

"Fall 2002 Field Trip Draws Large Crowd," Henry Ford Heritage Association Newsletter, 2003.

Ames, Herbert. From the files of the Detroit Economic Club, circa 1938.

"Fact Sheet: Dearborn Proving Ground Returns to Roots as Ford Airport for 'Taking Flight' Display." Ford Motor Company press release, June 9, 2003.

"Ford Convertible 4-Door Sedan of 1939." Ford News Bureau, #70637-A, circa 1950s.

Ford Motor Company. "Establishment of Factory Service Department." General Letter No. 1640, December 24, 1992. (From the files of the Benson Ford Research Center, Acc. 572 Box 30).

Letter from Erick Diestel to Charles E. Sorensen, telegram, Cologne, Germany, March 2, 1936, Review of 1936 International Automobile Exposition in Berlin (From the collections of the Henry Ford, HFM 0001890).

Marshall Bloom, John Tjaarda Collection: Papers 1900–1962. Detroit Public Library, National Automotive History Collection archives, Accession Number 6.

"Organization and Function of the General Motors Styling Section." General Motors Corporation brochure, date unknown.

Reminiscences: Joseph Galamb. Benson Ford Research Center, Acc. 572, Box 14 FMC, #11.12.3 V8 Galamb.

Reminiscences: Eugene T. Gregorie. Benson Ford Research Center. Interviewed by Dave Crippen in St. Augustine Beach, Florida, transcript, February 4, 1985.

Reminiscences: W. G. Nelson. Ford manager of Northern Michigan Operations. The Benson Ford Research Center, circa 1953.

Reminiscences: Frank C. Riecks. Benson Ford Research Center, circa 1953.

"Research Findings About Ford Werke under the Nazi Regime." Ford Motor Company, 2001.

"They're National Champion Auto Drivers." Ford News Bureau, circa 1940

Note: The holdings of the Benson Ford Research Center at The Henry Ford include the Ford Motor Company historical records. The collection includes parts drawings, photographs, sales literature, and other materials documenting the design, production, manufacturing, and sales of the 1940 Ford.

Index